Lighten Up!

A COMPLETE HANDBOOK FOR LIGHT AND ULTRALIGHT BACKPACKING

Don Ladigin
with illustrations by Mike Clelland!

GUILFORD, CONNECTICUT
HELENA, MONTANA

AN IMPRINT OF THE GLOBE PEQUOT PRESS

Falcon and FalconGuide are registered trademarks of Morris Book Publishing, LLC.

Text design by Josh Comen

Library of Congress Cataloging-in-Publication Data
Ladigin, Don.
    Lighten up! : a complete handbook for light and ultralight backpacking /
  Don Ladigin; illustrated by Mike Clelland.— 1st ed.
      p. cm.
    ISBN-13: 978-0-7627-3734-5
    ISBN-10: 0-7627-3734-4
      1. Backpacking. 2. Backpacking—Equipment and supplies. I. Title.

GV199.6.L34 2005
796.51—dc22   2005040338

Manufactured in the United States of America
First Edition/Third Printing

To buy books in quantity for corporate use
or incentives, call **(800) 962–0973, ext. 4551,**
or e-mail **premiums@GlobePequot.com.**

The author and The Globe Pequot Press assume no liability for accidents happening to, or injuries sustained by, readers who engage in the activities described in this book.

Contents

Acknowledgments

I wish to express special appreciation to Jim Blanchard and Michael Strong, co-directors of the Outdoor Pursuits Program of the University of Oregon for their encouragement and assistance in the preparation of this handbook. Jim proofread the manuscript making valuable suggestions and corrections. Many thanks also to Glen Van Peski for reviewing the early manuscript, and to Mike Clelland for his outstanding illustrations, which clarify and expand on the text.

—*Don Ladigin*

Foreword

Don Ladigin was "packing light" decades before most backpackers had ever heard the term "ultralight." My first acquaintance with Don was on a backpacking trip in 1975, back when large and heavy packs were the norm, and bragging rights went to the person with the most gargantuan load. We had agreed to car pool, so early on the first morning of the trip, our group met at the agreed upon meeting point in town. When Don arrived I was surprised to see that he had with him only a tiny pack, barely big enough for a day hike, yet only partly full. Apparently he had either forgotten his real pack or thought we were intending only a very short day hike. Always the mother hen, I inquired and was astonished to hear that the small sack on his lap was indeed his full pack. I was skeptical, to say the least, but it was midsummer, the weather conditions were mild and stable, the intended hike was an easy trail hike in nontechnical terrain not far from the road, and my assistant leader agreed that we would be able to provide whatever else Don needed. So, we allowed him to go, though with considerable trepidation. We kept a wary eye on him all the while, wondering what other odd behaviors we might witness, and curious as to how he would manage to stay comfortable at the near freezing temperatures that we expected by morning.

As it turned out, I've been learning from Don ever since. Instead of having to assist him, we spent much of the trip envying his light kit as we slogged under our towering loads of "essentials" and did our best to keep up to his pace. We had assumed that the small size of Don's pack meant that he might be ill-equipped, yet he had everything he needed and, adding to our chagrin, he was the only one in the group who had the tools needed to repair a participant's broken pack frame. Over the years I've led many trips with Don in the full range of weather conditions, in all seasons, from the Cascades to the Alps. He's completely at home in the wilds, where he's always relaxed, observant, and ready to assist others regardless of the conditions.

Don continues to amaze me and countless friends and students. He has led dozens of outings for the University of Oregon, assisting me in my work as director of the Outdoor Pursuits and Outdoor Leadership Training Programs. Participants on our outings must comply with extensive gear and clothing requirements, which often result in substantial pack weights. Don's become a living legend among local outdoors enthusiasts for his ability to comply fully with our stringent gear requirements while not exceeding the weight and volume of what most of us would consider a light "day pack."

A few years ago students on a snow-camping trip came to me to express their concern that Don's small pack might not contain enough to sustain him through the major snowstorm that was due to hit us during the second night of the outing. Needless to say they were even more concerned (and even I was a bit anxious) when the overnight storm dumped 26 inches of heavy Cascade "powder" on our campsite. Don was, of course, just fine, and as several of us were peering out of our half-buried tents at first light, his head erupted from the meadow where he'd been buried in his tiny shelter during the night. Before we could even get ourselves out of our tent, he'd brought us tea, and soon thereafter he was cheerfully scurrying about, helping others dig out from the storm.

Packing light requires careful planning (and a good measure of self-discipline) to assure that every item of gear and clothing is truly necessary, and that each item is as light as possible. On the other hand, packing light can make it possible to indulge in occasional whimsy. On a canyoneering trip in exceptionally rugged country, as our group prepared for unexpectedly cold, wet weather by dressing in fleece under rainwear pulled from our clumsy, heavy packs, Don astonished us by pulling a full wet suit from his impossibly tiny pack. By packing light he was able to afford the luxury of a wet suit while enjoying better mobility and safety on the slippery boulders and walls of the canyon. On a recent late-October backpacking outing, he arrived with his typical twelve-pound pack, which seemed impossibly small next to the thirty-five- to fifty-pound packs carried by most of the other participants. Two days later, camped on an alpine ridge during one of the first snowstorms of the season, the group members could hardly believe their eyes when he pulled a large plastic pumpkin full of Halloween treats from his tiny pack!

The most obvious benefit of packing light is, of course, a light pack. A light pack makes almost every aspect of outdoor travel easier, safer, and a lot more fun. And packing light may offer even greater advantages in the long term. Most longtime hikers, climbers, and backcountry skiers eventually suffer serious knee, hip, and spine damage, much of it related to their having carried large loads too often. With Don's help we now offer an "ultra-light backpacking" course at the University of Oregon, and we're pleased to see that lightweight gear and techniques are finally becoming widely popular among outdoors enthusiasts of all ages. Perhaps the next generation of backpackers, backcountry skiers, snowshoers, and mountaineers will be able to enjoy healthy feet, knees, and backs throughout a lifetime of outdoor adventures!

—Jim Blanchard
Director of Outdoor Pursuits
University of Oregon

Introduction

Lightweight backpacking is hiking and camping with everything needed to be safe, comfortable, and well fed while carrying a very small and lightweight backpack. In this book we will examine the most useful equipment and the techniques hikers can use to carry the lowest possible pack weight consistent with comfort and safety.

Hikers who gravitate toward lightweight backpacking tend to be highly self-reliant people who enjoy experimentation. Some use commercially available equipment, often modifying it to suit their needs, while others use custom-made or homemade gear. Almost every item of lightweight gear has evolved from conventional equipment and clothing. When a lightweight backpacker and a conventional backpacker lay out their respective gear side by side, both will have all the basics: a backpack, a shelter, sleeping gear, food, warm clothing, and miscellaneous useful smaller items. Item by item, the gear of the lightweight hiker will be noticeably more compact and lightweight than the traditional backpacker's gear. A traditional backpacker typically carries duplicate or redundant items. A lightweight hiker not only eliminates these redundancies but will maximize the usefulness of many items by using gear with multiple purposes.

So, there is really no mystery or secret to how lightweight backpackers achieve their light loads. Each item is deliberately smaller and lighter than the corresponding item carried by traditional backpackers, and any unnecessary items are deliberately omitted. The result is a much smaller and lighter load.

Some readers may be interested in achieving the lightest possible pack weight, while others might only want to reduce the weight they carry to a more manageable level. The information in this volume will be useful to both.

Most backpackers have realized at one time or another that they have overpacked for an outing. This realization may come in the middle of the trip when sore leg muscles rebel on a long

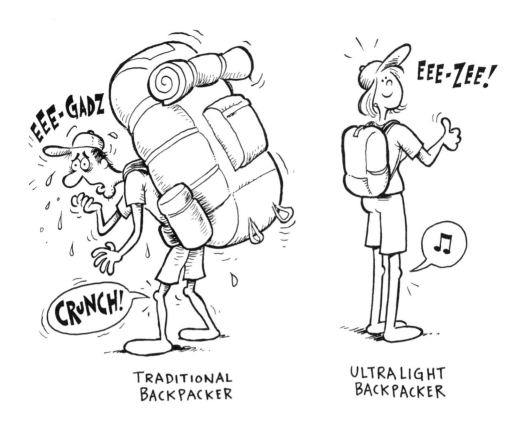

TRADITIONAL
BACKPACKER

ULTRALIGHT
BACKPACKER

climb uphill, or it may come at the end of a trip while unpacking large amounts of leftover food. Aside from what gets consumed during the hike, everything hikers put into a backpack will have to be carried for many miles, then carried back out again. Even small, light items will add up: Those many small weights become a single large weight once they're on a hiker's back.

Hikers who carry less weight spend less energy and can hike faster and farther when they want to. They will have greater agility fording streams and crossing slippery logs. If they stumble, they are less likely to fall, and when they do fall they are less likely to get hurt. A hiker who is less fatigued is more capable of helping others who are tired or injured. Hikers with interests such as photography or climbing are able to carry more of their specialized equipment when the rest of their gear is lightweight. A lighter load also allows the use of lighter boots, which save the hiker's energy and are gentler on the trail.

Hikers with lighter packs produce less impact in off-trail travel and are less likely to damage plants and soil, especially on slopes. Minimizing impacts on slopes requires avoiding delicate areas and may require taking somewhat more difficult route options, something heavily burdened hikers are less likely to do.

Some aspects of carrying a light burden are less obvious, but in the long run may be the most significant. When we are young, we can carry heavy burdens with little apparent effect on our knees and backs. However, carrying heavy loads can produce cumulative damage and result in serious impairment later in life. Besides, carrying a lighter load is just a lot more enjoyable!

There is no master list of lightweight gear that works well for everyone. You will have to experiment to find what light equipment works well for your particular needs. Be sure to use good judgment and stress safety while pursuing lighter weight. When trying out new or novel gear, try it in a safe environment, perhaps your back yard or a favorite campground, before venturing into the wilderness with it. If that's not practical, carry the old trustworthy gear in addition to the new gear until the new gear has proved it will work well. This is particularly important if the new gear is homemade or custom-made, since lighter-weight materials may be less durable, less weatherproof, or may provide less insulation than conventional materials.

ALPINE MEADOW (fragile surface)

ROCK (DURABLE SURFACE)

choose an ENVIRONMENTALLY RESPONSIBLE ROUTE!

Very experienced backpackers may be able to use some light-weight applications in winter camping or mountaineering, but the gear and techniques described here are more commonly used in mild weather and at low altitudes. Using lightweight gear in winter or at high altitudes is only for those with a great deal of experience and confidence.

PART 1

Understanding Lightweight Backpacking

Principles of Lightweight Backpacking

Computing Gear Weight

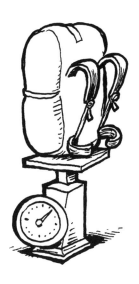

Principles of Lightweight Backpacking

1. Take enough gear to be safe, comfortable, and confident.
Lightweight backpacking is not about discomfort. It's about being comfortable with less weight on your back. The gear can be very simple and basic, but it needs to provide shelter, comfortable sleep, appetizing, nutritious food, safe water, and appropriate clothing for the conditions.

Psychological well-being is important too. It's important to have confidence in your gear. A gradual, thoughtful, step-by-step approach to lightweight hiking can develop confidence in your gear and abilities.

2. Know the actual weight of each item.
It is important to know the weight of each and every item that will go into the back-pack. When considering a gear purchase, you can find the approximate weight of an item by studying the catalogs and Web sites of suppliers. Manufacturers and dealers may underestimate weights, so the real story is only told when the item is weighed on an accurate scale.

C'MON BRO! CUT the HANDLE OFF!

2.95

5 lb. MAX
Battery operated

The best scales for weighing gear are postal scales designed for weighing letters and packages. Many of these scales have an accuracy of a tenth of an ounce, which is more accuracy than is really needed. A postal scale that weighs items of up to ten pounds is fine. Even major items such as sleeping gear or shelters for light and ultralight backpacking are not likely to weigh more than three pounds.

If it weighs TOO MUCH, find a smaller LIGHTER!

Many ultralighters use a notebook with descriptions of their gear and notations of weights. This makes it easy to total up gear weight without weighing the entire pack. One of the easiest ways to keep track of gear weights is to list the gear on a computer spreadsheet. This allows rapid sorting of items, with automatic totaling of weights.

3. Whenever possible, use multipurpose items.

A typical multipurpose item is a poncho, which can serve as both rain protection and pack cover at the same time. It can also serve as an emergency tarp, ground cloth, or privacy screen; its uses are limited only by the ingenuity of the backpacker.

SCARF NAPKIN WASHCLOTH

right on!

LENS CLEANER

SUN SHIELD UNDER a HAT

HANKY POT HOLDER SUNGLASSES CASE

A MULTIUSE ITEM!

A bandanna is another typical multipurpose item. It can be used as a napkin, handkerchief, pot holder, washcloth, scarf, lens cleaner, sunglasses case, and more. Like a poncho, a bandanna's uses are limited only by a hiker's imagination. Bandannas are usually made of printed cotton and are one of the few items hikers carry for which

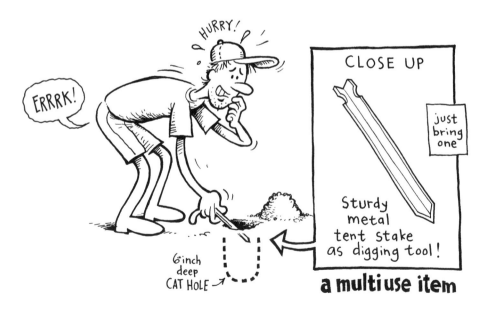

HURRY!

ERRRK!

CLOSE UP

just bring one

6 inch deep CAT HOLE

Sturdy metal tent stake as digging tool!

a multiuse item

the absorbency of cotton is welcome. Instead of the common orange plastic trowel, hikers can carry a single very sturdy metal tent stake to use for burying human waste. An item doesn't need to be ideal for all of its potential uses, it just needs to get the job done and allow the user to leave a more specialized tool at home.

Be sure the additional utility of any multipurpose item is really necessary and will result in less weight. There may be no advantage to having all the tools on a massive "multitool" unless those tools are actually needed and used.

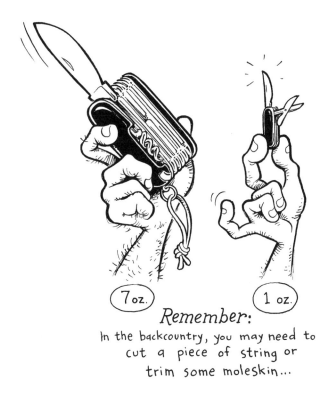

7 oz.   1 oz.

Remember:
In the backcountry, you may need to
cut a piece of string or
trim some moleskin...

4. Look at the heaviest items first.

The greatest potential for saving weight is in the heaviest items. The heaviest items carried by most backpackers are the backpack, sleeping system, shelter, food and cooking gear, and water.

CATEGORIES of PACK WEIGHT

5. When selecting gear, use the smallest items that will meet your needs.

Larger gear is proportionally heavier than smaller gear that may be just as effective.

6. Choose lightweight hiking gear that is useful, sturdy and dependable.

Judge gear in this order:

      Is it useful?

      Is it dependable?

      Is it lightweight?

      Is it compact?

If an item is not genuinely useful, not carrying it will, of course, save 100 percent of its weight. Gear that breaks down and needs repair on an outing is annoying and troublesome at best, and could result in serious risk at worst.

Computing Gear Weight

There are three distinct methods hikers use in calculating gear weights.

Base weight is the usual method used by light and ultralight hikers to describe the weight they carry. It is the weight of the pack itself and all the items carried in the pack that do not change in weight during the hike. Items that will be consumed, such as food, water, stove fuel, insect repellent, sunscreen, toiletries, and other items used up as the hike continues are not counted in base weight. This method comes from the tradition of long-distance hikers who replenish items that are consumed as the hike progresses. That's why consumables are not included. Most backpackers consider a base weight below ten pounds to be ultralight, and a base weight between ten and twenty pounds to be lightweight.

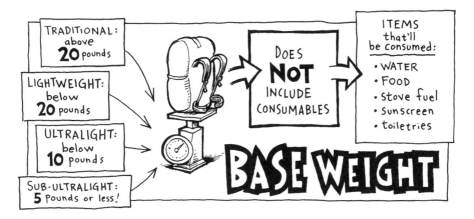

Pack weight is the method most often used by traditional backpackers to describe the weight they carry. It is the weight of the fully loaded backpack when the hiker starts out at the trailhead. This weight includes food, water, and all the other items in the pack, but does not include clothing the hiker is wearing or items in the hiker's pockets.

Both the base-weight and pack-weight methods leave out certain items, and neither has a definite convention for whether outside-the-pack items such as trekking poles are listed. So, when these items are carried, their weights may or may not be represented depending entirely on the preference of the individual. These irregularities are avoided by the "from the skin out" method.

From the skin out is another way to describe weight. It is the most complete but least used description of backpacking weight. It includes every item the hiker will be wearing or carrying as the hike begins. This is not the most convenient way to measure weight, but it does give the clearest picture of everything that is carried, including any items in the hiker's pockets

PART 2

The "Big Three"

Backpacks
Shelters
Sleeping Systems

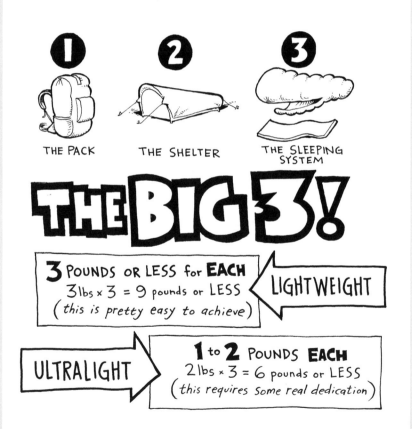

THE PACK　　THE SHELTER　　THE SLEEPING SYSTEM

THE BIG 3!

3 POUNDS OR LESS for **EACH**
3 lbs × 3 = 9 pounds or LESS
(this is pretty easy to achieve)　　LIGHTWEIGHT

ULTRALIGHT　　**1 to 2** POUNDS **EACH**
2 lbs × 3 = 6 pounds or LESS
(this requires some real dedication)

Backpacks

a simple ultralight pack

Backpackers transitioning from traditional backpacking to lightweight gear often can use their large old packs and simply put less gear or lighter gear in it. This makes sense from an economic standpoint. If backpackers already have a large pack and aren't ready to buy a new, smaller pack, they might as well use their old pack temporarily. Eventually, as their shelter and sleeping systems diminish in size and weight, large portions of the pack will remain unfilled and they can easily go to a smaller, lighter pack.

Lightweight Backpacks

Lightweight backpacks are smaller and simpler than standard backpacks, with fewer zippers and compartments. When empty, these packs weigh less than three pounds. Such packs can usually carry thirty pounds of gear comfortably: twenty pounds or less of gear, and ten pounds of food and water.

Ultralight Backpacks

The most useful kind of pack for an ultralighter is a "top loader." This is a pack with a single compartment that loads from the top. Many well-made small backpacks with a capacity of 3,000 to 3,500 cubic inches, often called day packs or summit packs, are excellent for ultralight backpacking. This kind of pack often has a flap or pocket that covers the top of the bag. There are very few things likely to break or go wrong with such a simple pack. Ultralight packs weigh two pounds or less.

Starting with a small pack ensures the pack itself will be light-weight and imposes discipline on the whole process of gear selection. A small pack makes it necessary to think seriously about compactness and light weight for every piece of gear that is chosen.

Many ultralight backpackers carry their small, light backpacks using just shoulder straps and feel no need for a waist belt. Others appreciate having a waist belt to take weight off their shoulders. Starting out with a small light pack that has a waist belt allows a hiker to experiment with carrying a pack both ways. It is much easier to cut the belt off a pack than it is to add a belt to a pack that doesn't have one. So unless you already know you don't want to use a waist belt, it's a good idea to start with a pack that has one.

One convenient way to transition to a small pack is to use an overflow sack. Such sacks can be pinched between the pocket and main body of many top-loading packs. An overflow sack expands the capacity of a small pack and provides fast access to such items as rainwear or an insulated jacket. It can also be hung from a tree to secure food from animals. The hand-sewn daisy chain keeps the sack from separating from the pack and getting lost on the trail.

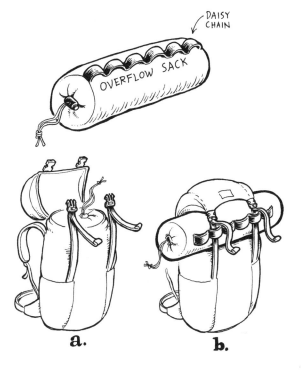

Shelters

Silnylon

Many lightweight shelters are made from nylon fabric treated with silicone. Hikers call this fabric "silnylon," but sil-nylon, siliconized nylon, and silicone-treated nylon all describe the same material.

Ordinary seam sealers won't stick to silnylon's slippery surface, so a silicone-based seam sealer has to be used for sealing seams on this material. McNett's "SilNet" is designed for seam-sealing silnylon and works very well. A glue syringe will use less seam sealer and does a neater job than the small paste brush that comes with the SilNet.

It's very important to remember that silnylon is not flame retardant. Shelters, ponchos, stuff sacks, and all other silnylon gear are highly flammable, so never expose any silnylon to flame or heat!

Tarps (Tarpaulins)

Tarps are versatile, lightweight, and compact to carry. They offer the best space-to-weight ratio of any shelter. Naturally, they're favorite shelters for ultralighters.

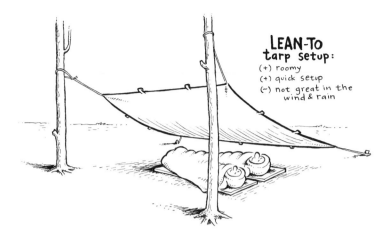

LEAN-TO tarp setup:
(+) roomy
(+) quick setup
(−) not great in the wind & rain

Tarps are not for everyone. Setting up a tarp to protect a camper in bad weather takes experience. Except for the pyramid set up, tarps are not as private as tents. For mosquito protection, some hikers add a fringe of no-see-um netting, but many ultralighters just wear their head net when mosquitoes are a problem. There are many ways to put up a tarp. The "bombshelter" setup with its taut ridgeline is exceptionally storm worthy in strong winds and heavy rain.

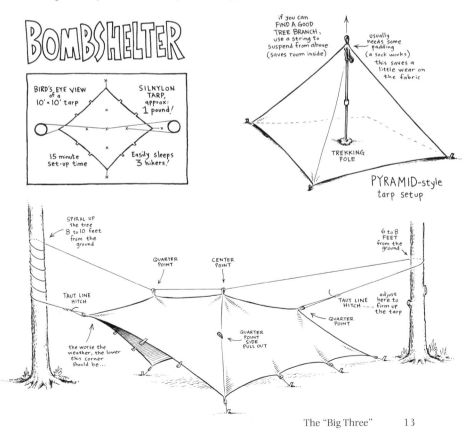

BOMBSHELTER

BIRD'S EYE VIEW of a 10' × 10' tarp

SILNYLON TARP, approx: 1 pound!

15 minute set-up time

Easily sleeps 3 hikers!

if you can FIND A GOOD TREE BRANCH, use a string to suspend from above (saves room inside)

usually needs some padding (a sock works) this saves a little wear on the fabric

TREKKING POLE

PYRAMID-style tarp setup

SPIRAL UP the tree 8 to 10 feet from the ground

6 to 8 FEET from the ground

QUARTER POINT

CENTER POINT

TAUT LINE HITCH

adjust here to firm up the tarp

TAUT LINE HITCH

QUARTER POINT

the worse the weather, the lower this corner should be...

QUARTER POINT SIDE PULL OUT

Tents

Tents are heavier shelters than tarps but they give greater privacy and more protection from the elements. A tent can be worth every ounce of extra weight when heading into an area swarming with mosquitoes.

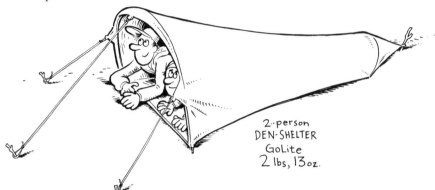

2-person
DEN-SHELTER
GoLite
2 lbs, 13oz.

Niche manufacturers make ultralight silnylon tents that weigh two pounds or less. Some of these small tents are rated for two people, but they usually are more comfortable for one person plus gear. Two average-size people could indeed fit inside, but every-thing except sleeping gear might need to be stored outside.

Two person tents are
CRAMPED!
(and heavy, too)

Ultralight-tent makers sometimes assume the hiker will have adjustable trekking poles that can help hold up the tent. The ability to adjust these poles precisely can be important to keeping such a tent taut. In some environments, finding a stick or a branch nearby to do the job well is unlikely. If you're not going to be carrying adjustable poles, it's better to use a tent that doesn't depend on trekking poles for support.

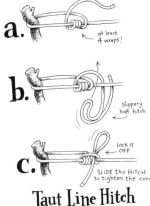

a.
← at least 4 wraps!

b.
slippery half hitch →

c.
LOCK IT OFF →
SLIDE this HITCH to tighten the cord

Taut Line Hitch

Most ultralight tents are single-walled tents. There is no liner to help manage condensation. When there is not enough air movement through these tents, condensation can form on the walls and ceiling. Much of this condensation comes from the hiker's breath, but perspiration and damp gear also contribute. Setting up near a stream or other very humid area when there's no wind nearly guarantees there will be condensation in the tent.

To cope with condensation in single-wall tents:
• Wipe down the inside of the tent with an absorbent cloth or sponge and wring it dry outside.
• Keep the tent taut. Sags in the tent will cause reduced headroom, which makes contact between condensation and clothing or the sleeping system more likely. It's worth getting out of the tent occasionally to tighten up the lines and keep all the panels taut.

H₂O VAPOR
DREADED CONDENSATION!

The advice "never use a stove in a tent" is especially important when using ultralight tents. The fumes from any type of stove can be deadly, and silnylon burns very readily.

Bivy Sacks (Bivouac Sacks)

Bivy sacks can be used in tiny stealth-camping spots much too small for any tent. There are two categories of bivies: bivies that provide complete shelter and bivies that are sleeping-bag covers and are not stand-alone shelters.

Bivies that provide complete shelter zip shut to enclose the sleeper in a tiny shelter barely larger than the sleeping system itself. Such a bivy will have a waterproof breathable top and may have mosquito netting and a hoop to keep the shelter off the sleeper's

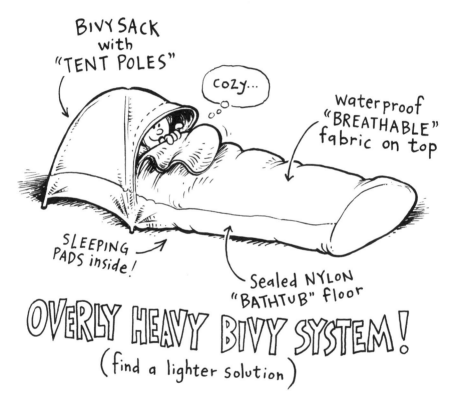

BIVY SACK with "TENT POLES"

cozy...

waterproof "BREATHABLE" fabric on top

SLEEPING PADS inside!

Sealed NYLON "BATHTUB" floor

OVERLY HEAVY BIVY SYSTEM! (find a lighter solution)

head. These tiny shelters may weigh two or three pounds, which is the weight of many ultralight tents. These bivies often develop condensation inside, especially when zipped up tight.

The other type of bivy has a waterproof bottom, a water-repellent, extremely breathable top, and can't be zipped closed. It is designed to have sleepers leave their heads outside of the bivy. This

If it's a nice night, there's no need to set up the tarp!

is much more refreshing than having your head confined inside the bivy. These bivies will protect the sleeping system from heavy dew-fall and even a few minutes of rain, but they need to have a tarp overhead in steady rain. Their virtues are light weight, around half a pound, and virtually no condensation.

In wet weather both types of bivies work very well with a tarp over them. A tarp solves the problem of getting into (and out of) the bivy without getting the sleeping system soaked.

Sleeping Systems

Sleeping Pads

Lightweight backpackers use the same closed cell foam and inflatable sleeping pads used by other backpackers. Usually the smallest, most compact gear is the lightest, but sleeping pads are an exception. Inflatable pads become very compact when deflated but are heavier than noninflatable pads. Closed-cell pads are preferable for lightweight backpacking because they are less bulky, more durable, don't absorb water, and offer much better insulation than open-cell foam pads.

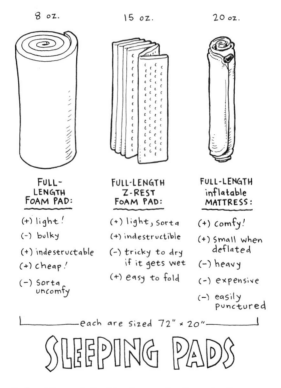

8 oz.   15 oz.   20 oz.

FULL-LENGTH FOAM PAD:

(+) light!
(-) bulky
(+) indestructable
(+) cheap!
(-) sorta uncomfy

FULL-LENGTH Z-REST FOAM PAD:

(+) light, sorta
(+) indestructible
(-) tricky to dry if it gets wet
(+) easy to fold

FULL-LENGTH inflatable MATTRESS:

(+) comfy!
(+) small when deflated
(-) heavy
(-) expensive
(-) easily punctured

└──────each are sized 72" x 20"──────┘

SLEEPING PADS

Packing inflatable pads inside the pack gives the best protection from damage, but lashing them outside the pack is also a common practice. It's a good idea to carry a repair kit for inflatable pads; eventually it will be needed.

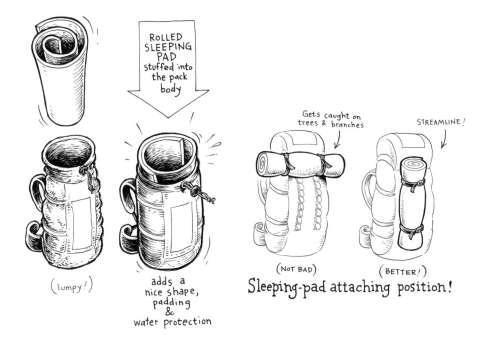

ROLLED SLEEPING PAD stuffed into the pack body

Gets caught on trees & branches

STREAMLINE!

(lumpy!)

adds a nice shape, padding & water protection

(NOT BAD)

(BETTER!)

Sleeping-pad attaching position!

Backpackers with "top-loading" packs can roll up their closed-cell pads and put them inside their empty pack, then stuff gear into the hole that is created as the pad unrolls by itself. This makes a temporary frame sheet, stiffening up even the most shapeless packs so they carry well. If this uses up too much space in the backpack, the foam can be rolled up and lashed vertically to the back of the pack.

Lightweight hikers usually choose three-quarter length rather than full-length pads, and they often trim a closed-cell pad to make it smaller and lighter.

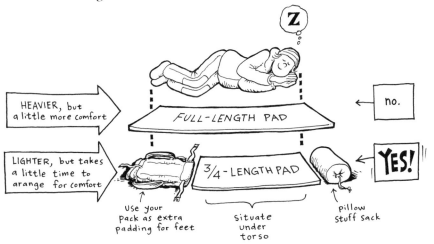

HEAVIER, but a little more comfort

FULL-LENGTH PAD

no.

LIGHTER, but takes a little time to arange for comfort

3/4 - LENGTH PAD

YES!

Use your pack as extra padding for feet

Situate under torso

pillow stuff sack

Sleeping Bags

Lightweight backpackers often use mummy-shaped sleeping bags made with down insulation. These bags offer lighter weight and a smaller packed volume than similar bags made with synthetic insulation. Some novice backpackers worry that down sleeping bags will get wet, which can reduce their loft. This concern is more legitimate for down-insulated jackets. A sleeping bag is relatively easy to protect from rain and dampness. It can be carried in a waterproof plastic bag and remain in the pack until it is protected by a shelter.

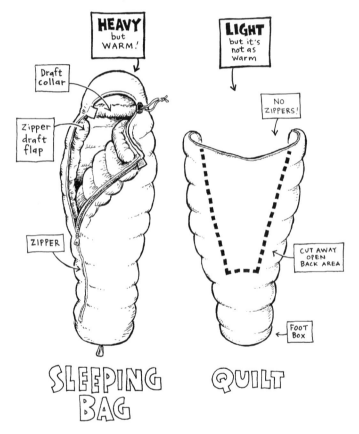

Quilts

The most common ultralight sleeping system uses a quilt instead of a sleeping bag. Quilts provide insulation over the sleeper where it does the most good, but not under the sleeper where much of the loft would be compressed by his or her weight. Quilts do have an insulated "foot pocket" that encloses the feet to keep them warm. Without a foot pocket, feet migrate outside the quilt and get cold. Quilts lack zippers, hoods, neck-draft collars, and zipper draft flaps. The sleeping pad underneath the quilt provides insulation from the ground and padding for comfort. Quilts can be made from breathable nylon and the same insulating materials used in sleeping bags, down, or synthetic insulation. Synthetic insulation is easier to work with but down quilts are lighter and more compressible. A damaged or unused sleeping bag can easily be converted to a quilt.

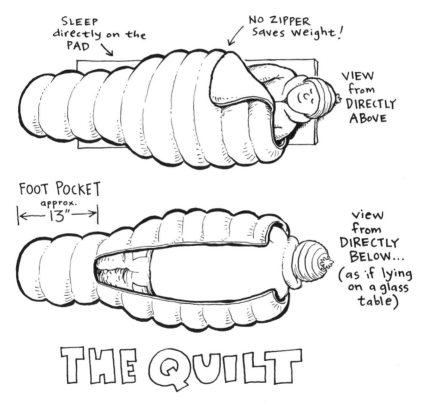

SLEEP directly on the PAD

NO ZIPPER saves weight!

VIEW from DIRECTLY ABOVE

FOOT POCKET approx. |←— 13" —→|

view from DIRECTLY BELOW... (as if lying on a glass table)

THE QUILT

Quilts work well for people who don't constantly toss and turn in their sleep. In warm weather they are easy to ventilate. For colder weather quilts can be pulled closely around the sleeper, eliminating extra space that otherwise would have to be heated up. Because a quilt doesn't have a hood, a warm hat (ideally with a chin strap) is needed

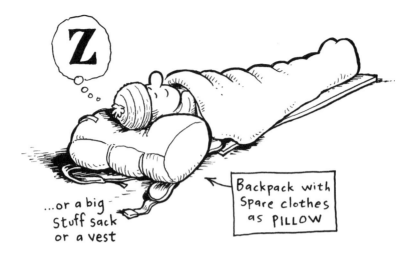

...or a big
Stuff sack
or a vest

Backpack with
Spare clothes
as PILLOW

in cold weather. Different people need different amounts of insulation to be comfortable under the same conditions. A quilt with 2½ inches of loft will allow an average or "normal" sleeper comfortable sleep down to twenty-four degrees F. A "warm" sleeper will be comfortable down to fifteen degrees F in the same quilt, while a "cold" sleeper may start feeling chilled at around thirty-five degrees F. If 2½ inches of loft doesn't sound like very much, remember that a sleeping bag's loft is computed by adding the lofts of both the top and bottom of the bag together. Quilts only have loft on top, so 2½ inches of loft in a quilt is the equivalent of a sleeping bag with 5 inches of loft. It is worth remembering that most women sleep considerably "colder" than most men, so women will need more insulation than men to be able to sleep comfortably.

Half Bags (Elephant's Foot)

Some ultralighters carry an insulated, hooded parka and a "half bag." This kind of sleeping system is also popular with some mountaineers for emergency bivouacs. Sleeping in the parka and half bag gives full insulation similar to a sleeping bag. This is a convenient system. The parka can be worn in camp, then later the half bag can be pulled up around the legs for sleep. In the morning the half bag will be packed up while still wearing the parka for warmth. When leaving camp to hike, the parka can go into the pack, and the hiker will soon be warm from hiking.

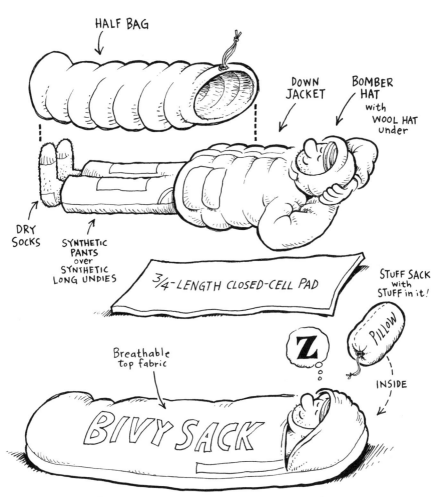

EVERYTHING INSIDE THE BIVY SACK

PART 3

The Efficiently Dressed Hiker

Clothing

Rainwear

Footgear

Clothing

Hikers expect a lot from their clothing. It has to insulate them from cold, ventilate in hot weather, and shield them from rain, snow, wind, and sun. A hiker's clothing has to do all this whether the hiker is moving and generating heat or standing still and cooling off. Lightweight hikers need to cope with these conditions while carrying only a few garments to minimize the weight and bulk of their pack.

Each piece of clothing should work cooperatively with their other clothing. Ideally, lightweight hikers should be able to wear all the clothing they carry at the same time comfortably, in layers.

For many years wool was preferred for camping and hiking clothing because it has some insulating value even when wet. Unfortunately wool is relatively heavy when wet and slow to dry.

Synthetic fabrics are softer and more comfortable next to the skin than the majority of wool garments. Most people find synthetics to be hypoallergenic. Synthetics also aren't eaten by moths, resist shrinkage, and are easier to clean than wool. But synthetics aren't perfect. Some synthetics promote odor, something wool doesn't do. Still, most hikers will be best served by fast-drying synthetic clothing with simple, uncomplicated, functional design.

your favorite wool sweater

Warm Hat

A warm hat is one of the most important clothing items any hiker carries. The best warm hats cover the ears. For even more warmth, the hat can also cover the back of the neck. Ultralighters using quilts will appreciate a warm hat that can be fastened under the chin. This will keep the hat from coming off when used with the sleeping system.

WARM HAT!

Sun Hats

A baseball-style hat will provide both sun protection and support under the unsophisticated hoods on ponchos. On the other hand, a fully brimmed sun hat offers more sun protection than a baseball cap and helps prevent sunburned ears and neck. This type of sun hat may fly off in strong wind unless it has a chin strap.

BIG SUN HAT!

WIND!

CHIN STRAP!

Torso Clothing

SHIRTS

Examples of effective clothing choices for the torso are a short-sleeve synthetic T-shirt, a long-sleeve synthetic zip-neck T-shirt, and a synthetic button-front shirt with convertible long sleeves. Each of these shirts can be worn alone as a hiking shirt in good weather, and they also can be combined in layers to deal with many different hiking conditions. Few garments are as flexible as a long-sleeve zip-neck T-shirt. When it's worn as an outer shirt, the long sleeves can be pushed up and the neck zipped down in warm weather. In cool weather the sleeves can be pushed down and the neck zipped up for more warmth. It can also be used as a long-underwear top under the button-front shirt, and at night it makes an excellent pajama top.

VEST OR JACKET

An insulated vest or jacket completes the layers needed for the torso. A vest is surprisingly compact, lightweight, and provides excellent warmth to the torso.

An insulated jacket is more bulky to carry than a vest, but the added warmth it provides for the arms is welcome in cooler conditions. The jacket will be used at rest stops and in camp but will usually be too warm to wear while hiking. Many ultralighters use their insulated jacket as a pillow at night. If they get chilled in the middle of the night, they can easily slip the jacket on to supplement their sleeping system.

Because it is both light-weight and very compressible, high-quality down is a favorite insulation of ultralight hikers. Extra care is needed to keep down dry in wet conditions. This is usually not difficult. The down jacket or vest and the sleeping system can be wrapped securely in separate waterproof plastic garbage sacks. This will keep them dry but will

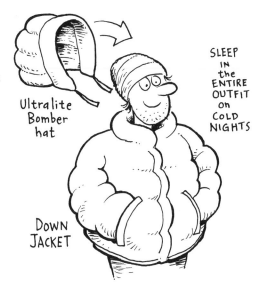

Ultralite
Bomber
hat

SLEEP
IN
the
ENTIRE
OUTFIT
on
COLD
NIGHTS

DOWN
JACKET

also keep them damp once they are allowed to get wet. If you're not certain you can safeguard down items from moisture, you may be better off using high-quality synthetic insulation.

Leg Layers

Most hikers find a "long john" thermal underwear bottom and a pair of synthetic hiking pants offer flexible protection for the legs, especially if the pants are convertible to shorts. Pants with zip-off legs are heavier than plain pants due to the weight of the zippers. Still, the versatility of convertible pants makes them worth considering in warm weather.

Legs stay warm while hiking, especially if there is little wind. Even in cool weather, one layer of thermal underwear under long hiking pants is usually enough leg insulation while moving. If the legs get cold while stopped, adding rain chaps or rain pants can trap enough heat to be comfortable, even in wind.

Whenever a lightweight hiker carries a second pair of pants, it should be sized to layer comfortably over the first pair.

Shorts

Hiking shorts are welcome in hot weather when bugs aren't biting. Many hikers use synthetic running shorts or soccer shorts instead of hiking shorts. These are lightweight and dry very quickly.

Gloves and Mittens

In warm weather at low elevations, carrying gloves or mittens is optional for the ultralighter. An extra pair of socks can be used as thumbless mittens, and small stuff sacks can stand in for overmitts (durable shells that fit over wool or pile mittens to keep them dry, usually made with waterproof palms and breathable, water-repellant fabric tops). This works as an emergency measure, but hikers are certain to miss the full use of their thumbs.

When cool weather is expected, having actual gloves or mittens is much more convenient and will only add a small amount of weight to the ultralighter's pack or pockets. Lightweight glove liners may provide enough insulation for an ultralighter's hands in cool weather. Hand coverings should not be small for the hands or have tight elastic at the wrists. Any tightness will restrict circulation and cause cold hands. In colder weather lightweight fleece gloves or mittens may be needed.

Overmitts alone are surprisingly warm. Overmitts are usually teamed up with mittens, but they also work well over gloves. This is a very flexible combination. The gloves allow good dexterity for camp chores, and when the gloves are layered under overmitts, the combination provides good warmth for normal hiking conditions.

ZONE OF FINGERS

WATER RESISTANT NYLON FABRIC

BE CAREFUL!

LOGO

THUMB AREA

Remove all logos and extraneous stuff to save weight!

NO INSULATION, Just a fabric Shell

Simple velcro cinch Strap

OVERMITTS
(aka: Mitten Shells)

SHELL worn OVER a pair of thin acrylic gloves

Socks

Socks may seem mundane and not very glamorous but they are one of a hiker's most important clothing items. Good hiking socks wick away moisture and provide the feet with warmth and cushioning with every step. Traditional hikers often wear liner socks under their hiking socks. In addition to wicking away moisture, these liner socks provide some "slip" between the foot and stiff boots, reducing blisters. Ultralight hikers using lighter, more flexible footgear usually are able to wear hiking socks alone, without liner socks.

Hiking socks need to fit the foot well. A sock that's too big for the foot will allow excess material to bunch up under the foot or at the toes. When this happens skin irritation and blisters can result. Socks that are tight or have tight cuffs will impair a hiker's circulation. Hikers with circulatory ailments will be affected even in moderate temperatures.

Cotton socks absorb moisture but dry slowly. Wet cotton socks stay cold and don't insulate. They also hold wetness against the foot, softening the skin and making blisters likely.

Pure wool socks wick moisture well but wear out quickly, especially at the heel and at the Achilles tendon where the sock rubs against the back of the shoe or boot. Adding synthetic fibers to these areas improves durability considerably.

Socks made with synthetic fibers or synthetic and wool blends are excellent for hiking socks. They wick moisture well and are tough and long lasting. When damp, or after they have been laundered, they dry much more quickly than either cotton or all-wool socks.

In addition to having at least two pairs of hiking socks, a separate pair of warm, dry socks used only for sleeping is a real treat when trail conditions have been wet all day. Changing into dry "sleeping socks" can be more than just a matter of comfort. When a hiker's feet have been damp and cold all day, it's important for foot health to provide a dry and warm environment for feet during the hours spent sleeping. For this reason, hikers should never sleep in wet socks.★

Spare socks have many alternative uses. They can be used as pot holders or emergency mittens. Joined with a few safety pins, a spare pair of socks can even make an effective headband to help warm the head and ears.

Not quite a mitten, but warm

Thumb in the heel space

SOCK AS A MITTEN

★The initial stages of trench foot can be avoided by having the feet warm and dry while sleeping. Trench foot can result if feet are exposed to above-freezing cold and wet conditions for more than twelve hours continuously.

Rainwear

Rainwear offers hikers more than protection from rain, wind, and snow. It offers great versatility when used to its full potential. Hikers can wear or sit on rainwear to keep from getting wet when sitting on damp surfaces. If a cloud of angry yellow jackets suddenly appears because their nest has been disturbed, hikers can quickly put rainwear and a head net on for protection from stings. Rainwear is effective at keeping heat generated by a hiker from escaping to the environment. When the weather is cold or windy, hikers can wear rainwear to take advantage of this warmth even when it's not raining.

SAUNA!

TOASTY!

[Rainwear when it's warm out]   [Rainwear when it's cool out]

Retaining heat can also have drawbacks. It's easy to overheat when wearing rainwear. Hikers can compensate for rainwear's warmth by removing some clothing layers before putting it on. Once underway, the rainwear's ventilation should be adjusted to avoid overheating. It's usually preferable to be slightly cool in rainwear rather than overly warm, which can quickly sap your energy.

Being slightly cool allows you to deliberately move faster to generate more heat if necessary. Overheating can cause a hiker's clothing to get wet from perspiration, which is just as uncomfortable, inconvenient, and dangerous as getting wet from rain.

Durable Water-repellent Coating (DWR)

Fabric manufacturers often coat the outside surface of breathable fabrics with water-repelling chemicals. This encourages water droplets to bead up and roll off the fabric's surface instead of soaking into it. DWR coatings are "durable," not "permanent." The coating works well initially but its effectiveness declines with use and laundering. Eventually the fabric will leak in areas where the coating has been abraded. The original factory DWR coating can sometimes be reactivated by heating the garment in a dryer or by gentle ironing. If this doesn't work, the fabric will need to have the DWR coating reapplied. This can be accomplished at home. Wash the garment with nondetergent soap, rinse thoroughly, and reapply the DWR while the fabric is still wet, following the directions supplied with the product.

Waterproof/Breathable Fabrics

Manufacturers use a variety of methods to produce fabrics that allow water vapor to pass through while blocking water droplets. These methods include laminating different fabrics and coatings together, and encapsulating individual threads with waterproof materials before weaving them tightly together into fabric. Lamination technology is decades old and has undergone steady improvement. More recent attempts to produce waterproof/breathable materials are still rapidly evolving. Whether using new or old technology, waterproof/breathable fabrics have limitations. They need to be clean; dirt and skin oils easily clog them. The hardest conditions for waterproof/breathable fabrics to deal with are conditions under which you'd like them to work the best: a downpour in an area of high humidity, with heavy exertion on the part of the wearer. Under those conditions you'll probably get damp despite the manufacturer's optimistic predictions. This doesn't mean the fabric has failed, it just means it can't cope with that much moisture all at once coming from both sides of the fabric. So, consider waterproof/breathable fabrics to be a work-in-progress. They don't offer miracles and there is still plenty of room for improvement.

Waterproof/Nonbreathable Fabrics

Light and ultralight backpackers often use technologically advanced gear, but for rainwear they sometimes use waterproof/nonbreathable fabrics, the simplest, lightest, and least expensive option. Rainwear made with nonbreathable materials needs to be well vented since no perspiration can escape through the fabric. If you are one of those individuals who doesn't perspire heavily, you're likely to have good experiences with nonbreathable rainwear. Just remember: Waterproof clothing won't let moisture in or out.

Wind Shirts

Wind shirts aren't technically "rainwear." They are made from tightly woven fabric and protect from wind while allowing perspiration vapor to escape. Since the fabric is tightly woven, these garments can resist occasional light sprinkles but will soak through in just a few minutes of sustained rain. Adding a DWR to wind shirts improves their ability to withstand rain but reduces breathability.

Instead of carrying a separate wind shirt, some lightweighters use their rainwear to block wind. This works but tends to be warm and trap moisture. Wind shirts can be very light and small: A wind shirt can weigh only three ounces and pack down to the size of an apple! Some wind shirt wearers use them with an umbrella, but actual rain gear is needed for secure protection from heavy rain.

Umbrellas

Umbrellas aren't exactly rainwear, but they can protect hikers from rain, so we'll deal with them here. Umbrellas may seem more appropriate for use in an urban environment than on a backpacking trip, but when you're not using trekking poles and there is not a lot of wind, an umbrella can be surprisingly useful. Umbrellas allow hikers to leave their rain hoods down, which keeps them cooler and allows for better hearing. Tarp users can stake an umbrella down at a tarp's opening to shield them from wind and

Good
Ventilation

BREATHABLE
WIND
SHIRT,
not true
rain gear!

the
Umbrella!
(a luxury item)

rain. Umbrellas can even be useful in fair weather. An umbrella can help protect a stove from wind, and in hot shadeless areas it can be used to provide shade while hiking or resting.

Nonfolding umbrellas are usually large, sturdy, and heavy. Folding umbrellas are smaller, lighter, and more fragile. Their small size is an advantage in brushy areas, where a larger umbrella would likely get shredded. Some small folding umbrellas weigh only six ounces and will fit into a pocket when collapsed, making them convenient to carry and access.

Ponchos

Rain ponchos usually have a simple hood whose function is improved by wearing a baseball cap under it. Simple and light-weight, a waterproof poncho can be used for rain protection or as a ground cloth, picnic blanket, emergency shelter, or for as many other uses as a hiker can think up. When used for rain protection, a poncho can be worn covering the pack in addition to covering the hiker. This gives good ventilation, since ponchos are loosely fitted rain garments.

Ponchos "flap" annoyingly in wind. When this happens there are two remedies, but unfortunately neither is ideal. The pack can be worn on the outside of the poncho, where its waist belt will reduce flapping, or the pack can be worn under the poncho with a belt or cord secured outside the poncho around the waist. Both methods reduce a poncho's normally good ventilation and trap moisture, which can make clothing damp from perspiration. Ponchos are not

RAIN PONCHO

as effective against rain as more fitted rain garments but are popular with lightweight hikers because they are so versatile.

Chaps

Rain chaps are the lightest and least bulky rainwear for the legs. They consist of two separate leg "tubes." Chaps made from silnylon are so light and packable that hikers can easily fold them up and carry them in their pants pockets. Rain chaps can be purchased ready-made but are an easy home sewing project for anyone with minimal sewing skills. It is convenient to have the legs wide enough so that you don't have to remove your footgear to put chaps on. The areas chaps don't cover can get wet, especially when climbing over obstacles. Chaps are usually used with a poncho rather than a fitted raincoat because a poncho can protect the areas not covered by the chaps.

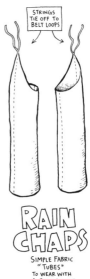

STRINGS TIE OFF TO BELT LOOPS

RAIN CHAPS

SIMPLE FABRIC "TUBES" TO WEAR WITH A RAIN JACKET

Fitted Rain Garments for the Torso

The design of fitted rainwear greatly influences its effectiveness. Well-designed rainwear for lightweight backpackers will have a sophisticated adjustable hood, excellent ventilation options, and should offer rain protection without unnecessary features that increase weight and bulk. Ventilation is vital for the torso regardless of the material used in the rainwear. Ventilation systems include two-way full front zippers, armpit zippers ("pit zips"), and core vents (mesh-lined pockets that can be opened to improve ventilation). Good ventilation is essential for a backpacker to be comfortable. A full front zipper should be covered by a storm flap with snaps. This gives a choice of using either the zipper, the snaps, or both, and if the zipper breaks during an outing, the snaps will allow the rainwear to function without

Oooh, VENTY!

PIT-ZIP

WEARING *EVERYTHING* UNDER
OVERSIZE RAIN GEAR*!*

resorting to safety pins or other emergency repairs. Velcro closures at the wrists are more versatile than snaps or elastic.

Rainwear will usually be the outermost layer of the clothing system and needs to fit easily over all the other clothing, including insulating garments. Don't be afraid to have the torso's rainwear a little large. Rainwear for backcountry travel should be about one size larger than outerwear used in town. A rain garment that is large for you may have sleeves long enough to also protect your hands from rain. For only a slight gain in weight, larger torso rainwear will be better ventilated, cooler, and more comfortable without compromising its effectiveness at shedding rain.

Rain Jackets

Rain jackets are short, usually ending between the waist and hips. They sometimes have a built-in hood and usually have a full front zipper. Because jackets are short, they seem lightweight, especially if they lack a hood. If you are expecting more than a few light sprin-

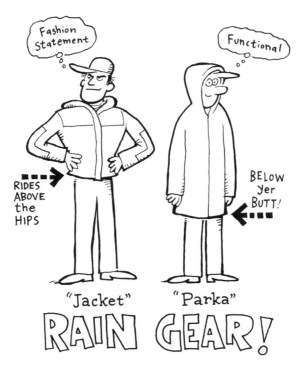

"Jacket" "Parka"

RAIN GEAR!

kles, a longer rain garment, one that covers the seat, with a hood is usually worth considering despite the small additional weight.

Anoraks

These pullover garments have hoods and often have a large "kangaroo" pocket in front. Anoraks are warm and snug jacket-length garments, well suited to cold-weather use. They are sometimes too warm for summer hiking because they can be hard to ventilate.

Cagoules

Cagoules are used more often by mountaineers than hikers. They are very similar to anoraks but have a "storm skirt" that can be untied or unsnapped and pulled down to cover

ANORAK

the knees or below. Cagoules are ideal for extreme conditions but are difficult to ventilate during heavy exercise.

Rain Parkas

Originally the word "parka" referred to an insulated pullover garment similar to, but longer than, an anorak. More recently, the term "parka" usually refers to a garment extending to about midthigh with a full front zipper and hood. Due to their length, rain parkas are slightly heavier than rain jackets but are worth considering because they provide excellent coverage.

Rain Pants

Unlike chaps, rain pants protect from waist to ankles. It is convenient if the pants fit easily over footgear. Full side zips make getting into (and out of) rain pants easy but also cause them to be heavy, stiff, and bulky. For that reason, lightweight packers usually prefer having only short zippers near the bottom of each leg.

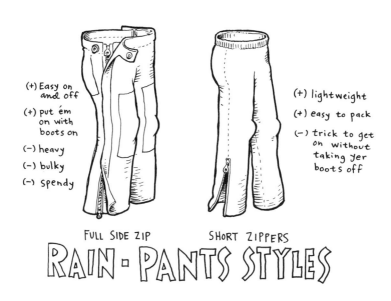

Cleaning Rainwear

Rainwear may only need hand-scrubbing and rinsing to be cleaned while the rest of a hiker's clothing, grimy from perspiration and trail dust, needs laundering. Many long-distance hikers wear rain gear while washing all the rest of their trail clothes in a Laundromat. A rain jacket and rain pants will look less out-of-place for in-town activities than a poncho and chaps.

Footgear

Good fitting, well-broken-in footgear may be the most important item a backpacker wears. When the fit is superb and the footgear is well chosen for the terrain, the miles seem to disappear effortlessly behind a backpacker, especially one carrying a light pack. Unfortunately, poorly fitted footgear can completely scuttle a hike. When footgear hurts your feet, every step can be a new misery, and your feet may take days or longer to recover from the experience! As a person walks or hikes, their foot starts at rest, is lifted and accelerates forward, then lowers and comes to a stop. This stop-lift-accelerate-lower-stop motion is repeated by each foot about a thousand times each mile and is what makes each pound of weight in footgear equal to carrying five pounds in the pack.

A backpacker can choose from many different footgear options.

Heavyweight Backpacking Boots

These sturdy boots (four pounds and up per pair) have been standard equipment for many traditional backpackers for years. They are high-cut and are usually made with full-grain leather. They are excellent for carrying a heavy pack over rough terrain. Durable and supportive, they need a long and thorough break-in period. Some backpackers claim such boots break their feet in to the boots, rather than the other way around! Very few light or ultralight backpackers will consider using this kind of heavy footgear unless they are headed toward exceptionally rugged, difficult, steep terrain.

Midweight Hiking Boots

Midweight boots (2¾ to 4 pounds per pair) are versatile, all-leather boots that are very popular with traditional hikers, who often consider them the best boots for all conditions. Lightweight backpackers sometimes use these boots for difficult off-trail travel.

Lightweight Hiking Boots

These light, inexpensive boots (2¾ pounds or less per pair) usually combine fabric (often condura nylon), with split-grain leather or suede in the uppers. This gives good breathability and allows them to dry quickly. Lightweight boots need little break-in time, and can feel comfortable right away, but they don't offer the same amount of ankle support that heavier, sturdier hiking boots provide. Unlike heavier boots, which can usually be repaired and resoled nearly indefinitely, when light boots become very worn, they are usually discarded and replaced with new lightweight boots. Lightweight hiking boots are often used by lightweight backpackers for terrain where lighter-weight low-cut athletic shoes don't offer enough support.

Athletic Shoes

"Boots" cover the ankle bone and will provide ankle support. "Shoes" are cut lower than the ankle bone and can't provide the ankle support that boots do. Hikers with strong ankles carrying light packs often take advantage of low-cut lightweight footgear, using running shoes, trail running shoes, "approach" shoes, hiking shoes, cross trainers, or other low-cut athletic shoes.

simple lightweight trail shoe

If you try using such low-cut footgear on hikes and find you are constantly "turning" or "spraining" your ankle, you'll want to use a more supportive lightweight boot for backpacking, at least until your ankles strengthen. If the terrain is challenging, or if low-cut shoes are not working well for you, try "trail shoes" or "day hikers." They are designed for lightweight packing and offer more protection and support than the lowest-cut shoes.

Sandals

Some hikers like sandals so much they would wear them year-round if they could. In some warm winter areas they do! A few sandal-loving hikers are able to use "trekking sandals," which have sturdy nonslip soles for both on- and off-trail routes. Hikers using sandals need very strong ankles, since most sandals give even less ankle support and arch support than athletic shoes. Most sandals also offer much less toe and upper-foot protection than boots or shoes. Bruised toes, cut and scraped

TREKKING
SANDAL

feet, and feet grimy from trail dust are par for the course, even if socks are worn with the sandals. If you're considering hiking in sandals, make sure they have sturdy heel straps and will provide enough traction for your route. Sandals do allow lots of air to get to your feet, but if you're wearing them to save weight, be aware that many sandals weigh more than athletic shoes.

Footgear Fit

It's worth taking all the time necessary to obtain hiking footgear that is compatible with your feet. This is true for all backpackers, and it's especially true for lightweight hikers. Many traditional hikers carry a second set of footgear, often lightweight athletic shoes

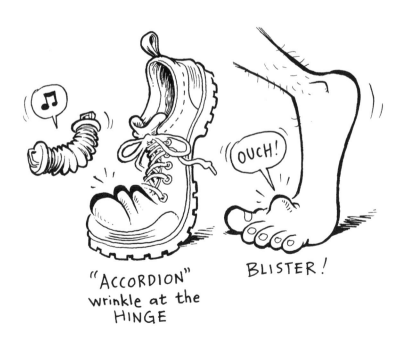

"ACCORDION"
wrinkle at the
HINGE

BLISTER!

or sandals, to use as camp shoes or for wading creeks. If their primary footgear gives them problems, they can switch to that second pair. Lightweight hikers seldom carry a second pair of footgear. This makes having comfortable, dependable, well-broken-in footgear doubly important. The easiest and best way to get a good fit in hiking footgear is to patronize a reputable outdoors store with a wide selection of hiking boots or athletic shoes. These specialists can measure your feet and make valuable suggestions for your footgear comfort.

There are also some things you can do yourself to give your feet and footgear the best chance of being compatible. I'll be calling all footgear "shoes," but the comments apply equally to boots.

When buying footgear, try new shoes on in the late afternoon or in the evening. Feet swell with use and are somewhat larger after being walked on all day than they are in the morning. Try new shoes on using the same hiking socks you'll be using on your hikes, since thicker hiking socks take up more room in the shoes and this makes a big difference in the fit.

Many people have one foot slightly larger than the other, and they should buy their shoes to fit the larger foot. Slip the shoes on and leave them unlaced. Stand up and slide your foot all the way forward until your toes hit the inside of the toe box. You should have enough room behind your heel to insert at least two fingers between your heel and the back of the shoe. This extra length is needed because new shoes will "shorten" after they have been worn for a while. Wrinkles will develop on top of the shoes where the toes bend, in effect shortening the length of the shoe.

Once you decide the shoes will be long enough for you, lace them up and wiggle your toes in the toe box. There should be plenty of wiggle room. Notice where your smallest toe is in the shoe. There should be no tightness there, and your smallest toe should be able to wiggle along with the rest of your toes. Now walk up and down an incline, if you can find one; otherwise kick the toe of the shoe firmly against a stationary object. Either way, the front of your toes shouldn't hit the front of the toe box, and the toes shouldn't feel squeezed at all when you do this. With the shoes laced up, you should not be able to lift your heel more than a

Extra room for the toes is essential!

quarter of an inch or so. If the heel lifts more than that, the up-and-down movements can cause blisters.

Breaking In Footgear

Fortunately, lightweight shoes and boots break in more quickly and usually give fewer problems doing so than heavier, stiff boots. Occasionally, lightweight footgear will work well straight out of the box, but don't expect that to happen every time. Before going on a long hike, you should break in even lightweight footgear. To do this, first wear them around the house, then on short neighborhood walks, including some hills, and then on day hikes. This will allow the new shoes to soften and shape themselves to your particular foot shape. Any problems with the shoes should become noticeable during this break-in period.

Lightweight footgear is less durable than heavier hiking boots. If you can feel sharp rocks at the instep and under the balls of your feet, the shoes are so worn out they are not providing enough underfoot cushioning, and they need to be replaced.

The Major Consumables

Water

Food

Water

At two pounds per quart, water is one of the heaviest items back-packers carry, and one of the most vital. It's needed for drinking, food preparation, and hygiene. If hikers had to carry all the water needed for even a brief backpacking trip, water would be the heaviest item in their pack. Fortunately, hikers usually can extract water from sources in the environment as they hike and don't have to carry all the water needed from start to finish. Unfortunately, back-packers can never be certain what is upstream from where they collect water. Drinking unsafe water will not instantly make you sick, but days or even weeks later, gastrointestinal illness can make you seriously regret your carelessness. To stay well, assume all water in the wild is contaminated, and treat it before drinking.

Waterborne Pathogens

Hikers depend on natural groundwater, which can contain a wide variety of organisms, some of which can produce serious illness.

Protozoa: At four to fifteen microns, these pathogens are relatively easy for filters to remove. It's difficult for chemicals to break down the hard-shelled cysts surrounding these organisms and attack the organism itself. Waterborne protozoa include giardia and cryptosporidia.

CRYPTOSPORIDIUM
(extreme close-up)

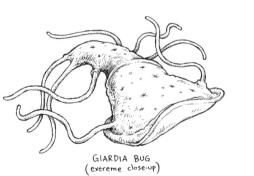

GIARDIA BUG
(extreme close-up)

Bacteria: Smaller than protozoa, these pathogens range from one-fifth of a micron to ten microns and are more difficult to filter out than protozoa. Waterborne bacteria include *Escherichia coli* (E. coli), cholera, salmonella, staphylococcus and streptococcus.

Viruses: Smaller than bacteria at four one-thousandths to one-tenth of a micron, viruses are too small to be removed by filtration. Fortunately, dangerous viruses are rare in North American waters. Unfortunately, viruses are common in the water of many third-world countries. Viruses found in water include polio, hepatitis A, and hepatitis B.

Making Water Safe to Drink

Water with silt or sediment in it should be clarified before treatment or filtration. Large numbers of bacteria cling to silt and sediment particles, and the particles themselves interfere with treatment and clog filters. When time allows, cloudy or silty water can be left undisturbed in a container for several hours to allow sediment to settle, after which the clear water can be filtered or treated with chemicals. If there is not enough time to allow particles to settle, the water can be coarse-filtered through a paper coffee filter. This will usually remove most of the particles.

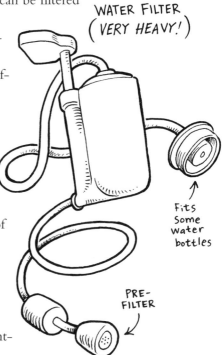

WATER FILTER (VERY HEAVY!)

Fits some water bottles

PRE-FILTER

FILTERS

Many lightweight hikers use a water filter because it is both convenient and effective. For one pound, the weight of a pint of water, they can enjoy the instant satisfaction a filter provides; just pump and drink. One water filter can easily provide clean water for several hikers, making a filter an especially attractive choice for light-weight hikers traveling as a group.

Filters work on a different principle from other methods of obtaining clean water. All other methods kill pathogens but leave them in the water. Filters remove pathogens and other particles from water, trapping them in the filter. Filters are mechanical systems and need regular maintenance to continue working well. Depending on the type of filter, the element will either need to be rinsed periodically or scrubbed to remove accumulated material. If the filter's element is not cleaned regularly, it can turn into a solid cake of green gunk and not allow water through at all.

CHEMICAL TREATMENTS
Iodine

Used by many backpackers during much of the twentieth century, iodine is still in common use, although more effective chemical water treatment is now offered by chlorine dioxide–based systems.

Iodine is effective against bacteria and viruses, but is ineffective against the protozoa cryptosporidium, which unfortunately is becoming more widespread in North America every year. Iodine treatment leaves water with a distinctive taste and color. Once the iodine has had time to destroy the pathogens, neutralizing agents or powdered vitamin C can be added to improve the water's taste. The instructions that come with iodine need to be carefully followed. There are health concerns associated with long-term iodine use, and pregnant or lactating women and individuals with thyroid problems should not use iodine at all.

Aqua Mira

Ultralighters often depend only on Aqua Mira, an effective chlorine dioxide–based chemical system that destroys pathogens including cryptosporidium without adding any taste to water. Aqua Mira can also be carried as a backup system in case a filter fails in the field. Whenever both a filter and Aqua Mira are carried together, the two systems work well in tandem for dealing with extremely suspect water. The filter should be used first, to remove large pathogens and particles that can interfere with chemical treatment, then the Aqua Mira should be used to neutralize those smallest pathogens that slipped through the filter.

little Cup PART A PART B

aqua mira

chlorine dioxide mix

ULTRAVIOLET LIGHT

Ultraviolet light is able to disinfect water effectively and quickly, killing protozoa, bacteria, and viruses. Small, lightweight handheld units are available, but as of this writing only a few backpackers have readily accepted this new technology. Backpackers point out that these devices are only usable with clear water.

Steri-PEN

(Agitate gently)

WEIRD BLUE LIGHT

Their reservations also include the expense of these units and some point out that the ultraviolet units don't fit conveniently into the mouths of many backpacking water containers. There also is a concern that these electronically complex devices could fail due to the rigors of backpacking. Despite these concerns, ultraviolet water purification is likely to gain wider acceptance in the future.

BOILING

When preparing soup, pasta, tea, and other food or drink requiring hot water, boiling is an excellent method of water purification. At low elevations, just bringing water to a rolling boil destroys any pathogens in the water, and if the water needs to be heated anyway, boiling it requires no extra time or fuel. In most other instances, stopping to boil water and waiting for it to cool to drinking temperature wastes fuel and hiking time.

Water Containers

Water can be carried in many different types of containers, from primitive to high-tech. Some materials are poorly suited to backpacking. Glass and ceramic containers, for instance, are heavy and breakable. Backpackers are occasionally seen with "bota bags" or canvas, aluminum, or stainless-steel canteens, but most hikers use plastic bottles.

examples of
HEAVY
water holders!

Traditional hikers seldom consider how different the weights for different plastic containers can be. The popular one-quart lexan polycarbonate bottles weigh between six and eight ounces each, depending on the manufacturer, the weight of the lid, and the wall thickness of the bottle. This means if a hiker using these containers wishes to carry four quarts of water, the empty containers alone would weigh nearly two pounds. Four quarts is the amount of water most hikers drink in one day, although in hot, arid areas hikers may drink as much as a quart every hour. Having the ability to carry four quarts doesn't mean that

much water will always be carried, rather it means whenever it is necessary, that amount can be carried. With a light pack, a hiker can collect a relatively large amount of water at the last water collection point before a "dry camp," a camp without nearby water. This allows hikers to choose an attractive, remote, and private overnight campsite with no nearby water source and still have plenty of water for drinking, cooking, rinsing trail dust from clothing, and bathing.

Plastic containers from juice, sports hydration drinks, soda pop, and other drinks are plentiful; Americans use four million plastic bottles every hour! Many of these bottles make convenient light-weight water bottles. After being used for a short time, these containers can be recycled and replaced by different bottles. Originally popularized by long-distance hiker and independent thinker Ray Jardine, two-liter soda pop bottles are very popular with light and ultralight hikers. Empty, these bottles only weigh two ounces and are tough enough to be used for many miles before being recycled and replaced by similar bottles.

The containers with the most to offer lightweight hikers are the soft water bladders used with hydration systems. These have several advantages over bottles. When empty they collapse and take up almost no pack space, and they are exceptionally lightweight. A durable beverage-grade polyethylene water container of this type with a two-quart capacity will weigh only one-and-a-half ounces. (Platypus water bladders are typical of this kind of container.)

One final suggestion about drinking containers: If you are carrying liquid fuel, use a fuel bottle with a completely different shape from your water containers. This will minimize the chance of drinking from the wrong bottle in the middle of the night.

Keeping Water Clean for Others

You can keep water clean for other users by using soap, including biodegradable soap, sparingly if at all, and making sure you are at least 200 feet away from any water source, such as a seasonally dry stream bed, before urinating, defecating, taking a sponge bath, rinsing clothing, or cleaning cookware.

Food

Food for lightweight backpackers should be tasty, nutritious, easy to prepare, and also lightweight and able to survive the miles without damage or decay. You'll also want to have variety; even favorite foods become tiresome after you've eaten them several days in a row. Food is heavy: Even lightweight low-moisture food will usually weigh between one-and-a-half and two pounds for each full day of hiking. That's the bad news. The good news: As food is consumed, the pack becomes that much lighter.

FIRST DAY HIKING...

LAST DAY!

MONDO HEAVY FOOD BAG

OoOMPH

TAH DAH

2 POUNDS OF FOOD PER DAY

EMPTY! STUFF SACK! (2½ oz)

easy math...
2 lbs. per day
x
10 days
= 20 POUNDS!

Start out with minimal PACKAGING and end up with less trash

Some hikers stick to a meal schedule of breakfast, lunch, and dinner, often with snacks in between. Others eat a morning meal and rely on snack foods until late in the day when they have a second full meal. Having many snacks throughout the day is a good way to keep the body supplied with energy, and many small meals are easier for the body to process while exercising. Hikers' appetites vary with the individual. Some hikers find their appetites diminish in the first days of a hike, while others have their appetites increased, sometimes dramatically. Be sure to bring enough food for the length of time you plan to be hiking, plus a little extra in case you don't finish as soon as you expect.

Food should be repackaged to reduce bulk and weight before reaching the trailhead. If you're using the bus, train, or especially commercial airplanes, it's a good idea to leave food in its original packaging until you've exited public transportation. Then you can consolidate your food for convenient carrying, and perhaps mark the bags with a magic marker so you know what's inside. Doing this after leaving public transportation will avoid lengthy explanations to officials who may examine your luggage and wonder what those strange powders are in your food bag. Hikers carrying high-moisture foods such as fresh fruit should plan to eat them early in the trip, preferably the first day out. This maximizes weight reduction and avoids spoilage.

EXCESS PACKAGING

ZIP LOCK

Dehydrated Food

Dried food can be purchased at many food markets and health-food stores, and many backpackers dry some of their trail food in a home dehydrator. Home preparation usually works well because it is relatively inexpensive and convenient. For instance, hikers can prepare double portions of their favorite meals at home, eat one portion, and dry the other for backpacking. Care needs to be taken

I'm organic!

HUGE BUSHEL

CHEWY!

ENTIRE HUGE BUSHEL

BIG & HEAVY

WASH & SLICE

DEHYDRATE

OFF HOT

TINY, LIGHT, & YUMMY!

to produce tasty meals. Removing too much moisture can result in tough, unappetizing food that doesn't rehydrate well on the trail. Removing some of food's water content makes it lighter, smaller, and less likely to spoil.

Freeze-drying (Lyophilization)

Freeze-drying is a complicated commercial process that removes virtually all the moisture in food without using heat. Food is frozen in a drying chamber, in which the atmospheric pressure is lowered with a vacuum pump. The low atmospheric pressure allows frozen moisture in the food to bypass becoming a liquid and slowly "sublime" directly to vapor without becoming liquid. When the food has lost nearly all its moisture, it is securely packaged to exclude air and moisture. If the package remains unopened, the food will remain edible for years. Freeze-dried foods are light but expensive, and not everyone enjoys their taste. Some hikers find freeze-dried meals that are supposed to feed two hikers are barely enough to satisfy one hungry hiker. Still, if you find freeze-dried meals that appeal to you and don't mind their expense, they are certainly light in weight.

"No-Cook" Food

One option that works especially well in hot weather is carrying food that doesn't require cooking. Food that can just be "assembled" and eaten is usually slightly heavier than food needing cooking, because it has higher water content. This weight penalty is small and on short trips it is more than made up for by not having to carry a stove, fuel, and cooking pot. Simple no-cook food is also perfect for when there's a big rain and wind storm and you don't want to light your stove, or when you're really tired from hiking and just want to eat quickly and crawl into your sleeping system and get some rest. Sandwiches of all kinds, nuts, chocolate, bagels, and cheese and crackers are typical no-cook foods. This kind of food can be surprisingly versatile. For instance, granola or muesli with nuts and dried fruit makes a tasty dry snack, and with powdered milk and hot or cold water, it also makes a substantial breakfast. No-cook meals don't need to be boring. Instant hummus powder mixed with a little water and some olive oil and spread on bread or crackers is one of my favorite trail meals.

Stoves

TRADITIONAL HIKER STOVES

White-Gas Stoves

Winter campers who need to melt snow for water appreciate the large heat output of white-gas stoves, but light hikers usually shun these heavy stoves, considering them temperamental, dangerous, and difficult to use.

Compressed-Gas Stoves

These stoves are simple and convenient to use. Some makers offer piezo-electric lighting, which makes them even more convenient.

Some compressed-gas stove burners and their built-in pot supports weigh only three ounces. These burners attach to metal cylinders containing a mixture of butane and propane gasses. Several different cylinder sizes are available for these stoves, and the total weight of the stove includes both the burner and the cylinder. Whenever possible, use the smallest gas cylinder that will be adequate for your hike. With thrifty use, some hikers can make the forty-five-minute burn time of the smallest cylinders last two or three days or even longer. These smallest cylinders weigh seven ounces when full and three-and-one-fifth ounces when empty.

ULTRALIGHT STOVES

Ultralight stoves are the lightest, simplest, and safest of the common stove types. These tiny stoves have no moving parts, so they are extremely reliable and easy to use. Ultralight stoves are also virtually maintenance-free, and they are completely quiet.

Trangia Alcohol Stoves

The Swedish firm Trangia has made a variety of sturdy stove and pot sets since 1925. The alcohol-burning brass burners for all the sets are virtually identical, but the associated pots and pot stands vary. The smallest and lightest Trangia stove sets are the "Mini Trangia" (Trangia 28) and the "Westwind."

mini Trangia 28 Alcohol Stove

Other Alcohol Stoves

In addition to Trangias, there are many other alcohol stoves. Some of these stoves are commercially made, while others can be home-made from directions found on the Internet using aluminum cans that can be found at any supermarket. If you experiment with making your own alcohol stove, don't forget that in addition to the stove itself, you will need a pot stand to hold the pot above the stove.

A couple of important safety notes regarding all alcohol stoves:

Vargo Triad titanium Alcohol Stove

1. Burn only alcohol fuel, never gasoline.
2. Alcohol flames are easy to see at night, but may be invisible in daylight. For safety, be sure your alcohol stove isn't burning before you move it or add fuel to it.

The Esbit Stove (pocket stove)

The Esbit stove is a cleverly designed German stove that burns solid fuel tablets. Closed up, the Esbit stove measures 3 inches by 4 inches by ¾ inch, and weighs three-and-one-quarter ounces. It's called a "pocket stove" because its small size makes it easy to slip

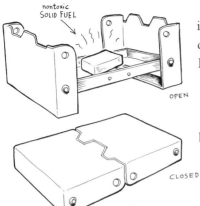

nontoxic
SOLID FUEL

OPEN

CLOSED

into a pocket. Six of the solid fuel tabs can be stored inside the closed stove. Each half-ounce fuel tab will bring a pint of water to a rolling boil in about eight minutes, with some of the tab unconsumed. The fuel tablet can be blown out when the water is hot, and what's left of the tab can be used again.

Esbit fuel tablets can be hard to light, so some hikers put a spot of fire starter on one corner of the tab and light it there. Burning tabs need to be protected from wind. It is helpful to rig up a windscreen of aluminum foil around the stove and pot to increase the Esbit stove's efficiency. Esbit stoves can also burn less-expensive fuel tablets such as Trioxane, from surplus stores, and other non-Esbit fuel tablets. These less-expensive tabs leave a messy residue in the stove and don't burn as hot as genuine Esbit fuel. Esbit fuel tabs burn well even at high altitudes and at below-freezing temperatures.

Half open
with a
cup
(like a
Sierra cup)

Full open
with
pot

in use...

While Esbits are good stoves for a single person, a more powerful stove, such as a compressed-gas stove, is a better choice if it will be shared by several people.

Pots

The shape of a pot makes a difference in how well it will work for backpacking. A skinny, tall pot is much more likely to tip over, wasting its contents and the fuel used to make its contents hot. Skinny pots are also more likely to have flames from a stove reach-

LID increases efficiency

LID also works as FRY PAN

SHORT & WIDE, efficient on a stove

easy to TIP OVER!

TALL & NARROW inefficient on a stove

ing up the sides of the pot, which is not an efficient method for heating the contents. A fat, squat pot can capture more heat from the flame under it, as well as being more stable. Gently rounded corners at the bottom of a pot make the pot easier to clean.

Most lightweight backpackers don't do "fancy" cooking. If you plan to have typical backpacker's "one pot" meals, a single lightweight saucepan should be plenty. A one-quart pot is a good choice for a single hiker, and a two-quart pot is usually large enough for two or three people. Pots should be covered when heating water or food, to increase efficiency. A lightweight aluminum lid or even a tinfoil "lid" will keep cooking time to a minimum and save fuel.

If you are not doing anything more elaborate than heating water, you might not need a pot at all. Aluminum or titanium cups or mugs are lightweight and will work very well for heating water for a single person. Another alternative to a pot is a lightweight one-quart tea kettle, which can heat water even more efficiently than a pot.

If you want to be able to sautè, you can carry a pot with a lid, which doubles as a frying pan and is coated with a nonstick surface. This will allow you to make pancakes and all other fried foods conveniently. Frying usually generates more cooking smells than other cooking methods. This can draw wildlife to

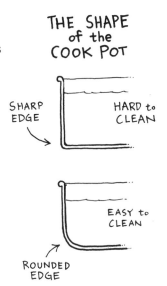

THE SHAPE of the COOK POT

SHARP EDGE

HARD to CLEAN

EASY to CLEAN

ROUNDED EDGE

your cooking site. When this is a concern, prepare fried food away from your campsite and your food-storage area.

POT MATERIALS

The material from which a pot is made makes a difference in how much it weighs and how well it cooks. For instance, cast-iron cookware cooks food well and retains heat after being removed from the flame, but its weight relegates it to car campers and mule trains. Stainless-steel cookware has the advantage of not rusting, but it is relatively heavy for lightweight packing and doesn't conduct heat as well as aluminum. Aluminum and titanium are favorite materials for light and ultralight backpacking pots. A titanium pot can be very lightweight because titanium is strong even when it is very thin. Titanium pots are excellent for heating water. If you're cooking food in a titanium pot, keep stirring and keep a close watch-the thin metal has a tendency to scorch and burn foods. Aluminum is an excellent conductor of heat and cooks food evenly and well. Uncoated aluminum cookware can react with acidic foods such as tomatoes, but if it has a nonstick coating, this problem is eliminated and the aluminum pot will be very easy to clean. Aluminum cookware that has been "hard-anodized" is available, and the hard-anodizing acts as a nonstick coating. Hard-anodizing puts a thin coating over aluminum that is harder than stainless steel. Hard-anodized aluminum cookware is highly recommended if you're going to cook using an aluminum pot.

Adding Hot Water to Food

The simplest hot backpacking meals only require hot water. This is not as limiting as it might sound. With hot water you can reconstitute all sorts of dry and freeze-dried meals, make tea, coffee, hot chocolate, and other hot drinks, as well as soup and hot cereal. If the food is in a freezer-storage ziplock bag,★ hot water can be added to the bag and ten minutes later the meal can be eaten directly from the bag with a spoon. The only item that will need

---

★Freezer storage bags are tougher and safer to use than ordinary plastic bags.

it's all organic!

CHOMP!

GRANOLA, OATS, DRIED FRUIT & POWDERED MILK (add HOT water)

Hanky as "POT HOLDER"

You can prepare HOT FOOD with HOT WATER!

USE A ZIPLOCK BAG as yer bowl!

cleaning is the spoon. The used plastic bag can be used to hold garbage to be packed out.

Boil-in-bag Cooking

If you want to cook an omelet but don't have a frying pan, you can always use the boil-in-bag method of cooking. Put the eggs and other ingredients into a plastic freezer-storage bag, close the bag securely, and heat the bag in boiling water until the eggs are no longer runny. When it's done you can eat the omelet directly from the bag with a spoon. This method makes no mess and generates few cooking smells to attract animals. Some backpackers like this method so much they use it at home! Other foods can be prepared with this method, but omelets are the most common preparation.

Steam Baking

Steam baking is completely different from baking with a reflector oven or baking at home with a conventional oven. Steam baking is a way to prepare baked foods without using a lot of fuel. Any kind of cookies, muffins, biscuits, or bread can be baked quickly and easily using this method. Baking with steam only requires a standard pot and lid, and a perforated shelf of any sort to hold the batter containers above the boiling water, which produces steam. The batter containers can be any lightweight metal container. Aluminum muffin cups or tart tins work well. You don't need a large pot for

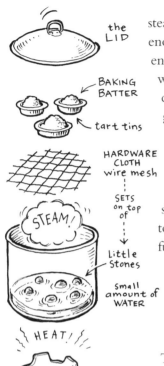

the LID

BAKING BATTER

tart tins

HARDWARE CLOTH
wire mesh

SETS on top of

STEAM!

Little Stones

Small amount of WATER

HEAT!

STOVE

STEAM BAKING

steam baking. Any pot will work if it is wide enough to accept the batter containers, and tall enough to keep the batter containers above water in the bottom of the pot. Several small containers will bake more quickly than a single large container. Fill your batter containers only two-thirds full, since the batter will expand as it cooks. Containers that are completely full at the start of baking will overflow. Place the batter containers on the shelf, cover the pot, and heat it. Allow steam to fill the pot. After five or six minutes, carefully open the pot, allow the steam to escape, and stick a toothpick into the middle of the baking goods. If the toothpick comes out clean, the baking is finished. If some batter clings to the toothpick, a few more minutes of steam will be needed.

There are a few points to keep in mind when steam baking. If you use a packaged mix, use one that doesn't require eggs to be added. The eggs should already be in the mix. Otherwise, you'll need to add eggs, which is not always easy in the field, or you'll need to add powdered eggs to the mix in the correct equivalent of the fresh eggs called for in the directions. Baked goods produced by steam baking come out nicely "moist," and never overly dry. It's hard to burn anything with this method, even if you leave what you're baking in the pot after it's done baking. You can't "brown" the baked goods or make them crisp with this method, but most baked goods prepared by steam baking come out well and are a welcome treat.

Safeguarding Food

When you leave food unprotected, you are inviting the birds and animals of that area to help you eat it. If you are only leaving some food out for a few minutes, keeping it inside a cooking pot with the lid on securely should protect it from small rodents, but this won't protect food from animals larger than mice. One lightweight approach to securing food from animals up to the size of raccoons is using a clean, new one-gallon paint can. Such cans can be purchased new and unused from many paint stores, and they have excellent tight-fitting lids. These cans usually need to be painted on the outside to keep them from rusting.

CRITTER-PROOF FOOD STORAGE

ODOR-BARRIER BAGS

Special plastic bags that don't allow food smells to escape are lightweight and effective at keeping very "odorous" food from being detected by smell. Don't try this with ordinary plastic bags—these bags are specifically manufactured as "odor-barrier" bags. Using odor-proof bags, and making certain no food particles or smells contaminate the outside of the bags, greatly increases the effectiveness of other food-safeguarding methods.★

ANIMAL-RESISTANT FOOD SACKS

To protect food from animals, tough, tear-resistant food bags made from Aramid "bulletproof" fibers are available commercially. The effectiveness of these bags can be enhanced by using them in conjunction with odor-barrier bags. These animal-resistant bags are lighter and more convenient to carry than hard-shell protective bear canisters. As food is used up, these soft bags will need progressively less volume in the backpack. Unfortunately, if a bear becomes interested in one of these bags, even if the bag does not get torn open, the bag's contents can be pulverized by the bear's efforts. As of this printing, such food sacks are not approved for use in problem hiking areas where bears have been habituated to associating hikers with easy-to-obtain food.

★Made by Watchful Eye designs, these patented Odor Proof bags are airtight and waterproof to 200 feet.

HANGING FOOD

If you plan to hang your food to keep it safe, you'll need 40 to 50 feet of cord in addition to the cord needed for your shelter. The method illustrated is called the PCT (Pacific Crest Trail) method. It will usually keep food safe from animals, including bears, in most areas. No method of hanging food can be depended on to keep food safe in areas where bears associate campers with food. In those areas you'll need a bear canister, as these bears have learned ways to defeat even the cleverest hanging systems.

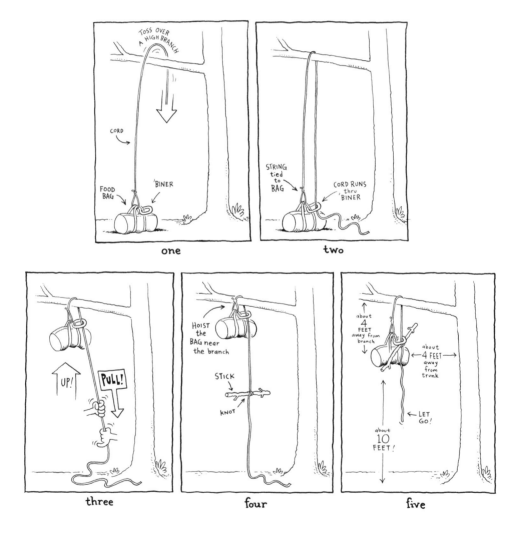

one

two

three

four

five

BEAR CANISTERS

When visiting an area where problem hikers have allowed bears to associate people with easy-to-acquire food, a bear canister or "bear can" is the most effective way to safeguard food, and may be legally required. A bear can has to be too large for a bear to be able to carry it away in its mouth, so the lightest canister weighs nearly two pounds. A bear may knock the canister around for a while before it loses interest in it, so the canister has to be left in an area where it can be found easily if it has been moved.

BEAR-PROOF
CANISTER

WHERE TO LEAVE
the
BEAR CAN
overnight

LOW AREA or DEPRESSION,
but not a stream-course

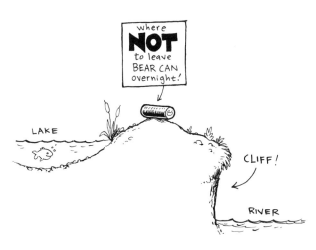

where
NOT
to leave
BEAR CAN
overnight!

LAKE

CLIFF!

RIVER

PART 5

The Small Necessities

Miscellaneous

Miscellaneous

These miscellaneous items are small, lightweight, and indispensable.

Matches

For quickly and dependably lighting a stove or starting a fire, matches are simple and lightweight. They are hard to beat. There are two general classes of matches: ordinary paper or wooden household matches, and "emergency" matches. The ordinary inexpensive household matches work well in good weather as long as they are carried in a waterproof container. Even a book of paper matches carried in a ziplock plastic bag works well for camp chores in good weather, as does an inexpensive cigarette lighter.

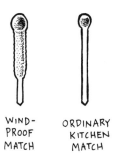

Emergency matches are a world apart from ordinary matches. Variously named "storm," "stormproof," "hurricane," "cyclone," "waterproof," "weatherproof," or "lifeboat" matches, these expensive supermatches are distinguished by having a very long match head. Once they have been struck on an abrasive surface, these amazing matches can even be completely submerged in water and will continue to burn until the match head is consumed! A dozen or so of these emergency matches should be carried in a waterproof container by every hiker. Since they are expensive, emergency matches should be saved for genuine emergencies and inexpensive ordinary matches used for ordinary camp tasks.

WIND-PROOF MATCH   ORDINARY KITCHEN MATCH   CHEAPO tiny lighter

Fire Starter

Fire starter is seldom needed, but when a fire is really needed, it's usually in terrible weather and every bit of help is welcome. Having fire starter can make the difference between starting a fire easily and striking match after match in a futile attempt to get a fire going.

There are many excellent commercial fire starters on the market, and they all do the job well. One type squeezes out of a tube like toothpaste. This paste can even be put on the end of a twig or stick, lighted, and then used as a long match.

An effective fire starter can also be made inexpensively at home from cotton balls and white petroleum jelly and carried in a 35mm-film canister. Wash the film canister with soap and water to rid it of any chemical residue from the film and dry it thoroughly. Saturate the cotton balls with white petroleum jelly and store them in the film container. When you need fire starter, pull one of the cotton puffs apart and light it with a match. These petroleum-saturated cotton puffs burn surprisingly long and hot. In addition to being a fire starter, the white petroleum jelly in the puffs can be used to soothe minor scrapes and chapped lips.

Nylon Cord (50 feet)

Parachute cord or other thin strong cord is needed for many different purposes: erecting a tarp or tent, running to tent stakes, hanging food. It can even be used to replace broken shoelaces.

Knife

A small sharp knife of any type is useful for cutting food and parachute cord and for many other camp chores. It needn't be large or heavy. A small, folding pocketknife is perfectly adequate.

Compass

Two kinds of compasses are used by backpackers: the simple baseplate or "protractor" compass and the more complex "sighting" compass, which often has a mirror. If you need a mirror for your contact lenses or to do intimate personal "tick checks," you may find the mirror useful. Otherwise the simpler baseplate compass is all you'll need, and it's less expensive too! Either way, a good backpacking compass will have:

Simple COMPASS

WORKS GREAT!
Do you really need
anything more complex?

- 1- or 2-degree graduations.
- a liquid-filled compass housing to minimize needle swing.
- adjustable declination.
- luminous points for night use.

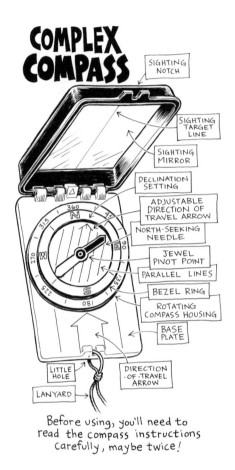

COMPLEX COMPASS

SIGHTING NOTCH

SIGHTING TARGET LINE

SIGHTING MIRROR

DECLINATION SETTING

ADJUSTABLE DIRECTION OF TRAVEL ARROW

NORTH-SEEKING NEEDLE

JEWEL PIVOT POINT

PARALLEL LINES

BEZEL RING

ROTATING COMPASS HOUSING

BASE PLATE

LITTLE HOLE

DIRECTION -OF -TRAVEL ARROW

LANYARD

Before using, you'll need to read the compass instructions carefully, maybe twice!

Map

Topographic maps are essential for most backcountry travel. A 7.5-minute USGS (United States Geological Survey) map is a good choice. Keep it where you can refer to it quickly and easily. Look backwards as well as forwards and relate what you're seeing to the map. Notice drainages and other obvious landmarks, and predict what is coming up next. Relating your observations of the terrain to the features shown on the map will keep you from getting lost.

Hygiene Kit

Backpackers are usually better off with unscented toiletries. Toiletries with scents are more common and easier to find than their unscented counterparts but can be mistaken for food by animals.

Toiletries with scents should be protected from loss in the same way food items are safeguarded.

ORAL HYGIENE

Oral hygiene necessities include:
- floss
- toothbrush with bristle cover
- toothpaste or tooth powder

Backpackers need to brush and floss on the trail just as they do at home. Unscented (unflavored) floss is preferable and can also be used as a tough thread for gear repair if you carry a needle with a large enough eye. An unaltered standard toothbrush is fine; even ultralighters seldom bother to drill holes in toothbrush handles or shorten them, as doing so saves very little weight. The only reason to slightly shorten a toothbrush handle would be to make it fit into a ditty bag with the rest of your hygiene items. A toothbrush bristle cover is useful since without it the bristles can become damaged.

Mechanical scrubbing with the toothbrush does much of the work cleaning teeth and gums, but most backpackers also use conventional toothpaste. Ultralighters often prefer tooth powder because it's lighter. Only very small amounts of toothpaste or tooth powder are needed, transferred to a tiny container, so the total weight difference between paste and powder is very small, at least for short trips.

For emergency relief from a toothache on the trail, a dental "poultice," designed to reduce toothache pain, is very lightweight. Oil of cloves is an effective dental anesthetic, and even a single clove can be held against a sore tooth to give some relief from pain.

BIODEGRADABLE SOAP

Staying clean and fresh on the trail is more of a challenge than it is at home, but it's worth the trouble. If you're in an area with abundant water, remember to bathe far from lakes or streams to avoid contaminating pristine waters. This means you'll need to carry water at least 200 feet away from water sources, as ground water flow can carry pollutants long distances. For drying, microfiber towels are small and light. They absorb large amounts of water, can be wrung out to lose most of their moisture, and they dry very quickly. If it's a hot day, the natural temperature of the water may be refreshing. If the water needs to be warmed to be usable, being very slightly heated to lukewarm usually allows it to be used comfortably. If soap is used at all, just the tiniest bit of biodegradable soap is plenty. Even biodegradable soap should be used extremely sparingly in wild areas.

Reducing Bacteria

In addition to washing, another strategy for controlling odor is reducing the amount of bacteria on the skin. Some hikers carry a few povidone-iodine prep pads or a small (one- or two-ounce) plastic bottle of liquid povidone-iodine, a broad-spectrum microbicide, in their first-aid kits.* This is usually used for cleaning minor wounds but is also extremely effective at reducing armpit or foot odor. When used to control odor, the povidone-iodine is wiped on the area, allowed to remain on the skin for three minutes or so, and then rinsed off with plain water. If it's not rinsed off, the iodine it contains will stain clothing. After this treatment it will take time, sometimes several days, for bacteria to reestablish a presence on the skin surfaces that have been treated and cause odor again.

HAND WASHING

Hikers should wash their hands thoroughly with soap and water after defecation or urination, and before touching food.

FOOT WASHING

Bacteria love dark, moist, warm environments. Shoes and boots create this environment perfectly! If it's warm enough to do so comfortably, wash and dry your feet at night before getting into your sleeping system. Before going to bed, many hikers launder the pair of socks they have worn all day at this time. The next day they will hike using a different pair of socks, giving the freshly laundered pair all day to dry. Shoe inserts that combat odor work well on hikes,

---

*Betadine solution is a common antiseptic microbicide and works well for first-aid and odor control.

Two-liter plastic Soda bottle

BANDANNA
- or -
Small microfiber
towel
(very absorbent)

STINKY!

BIODEGRADABLE
SOAP
(use only
one
drop!)

wash socks
if you
need to...

but you'll need to remove them from shoes before wading creeks—getting the inserts soaking wet reduces their effectiveness.

Toilet Paper

If you use toilet paper instead of using natural materials, you should pack used toilet paper out in a plastic bag. Don't bury it, as it is likely to be dug up by animals. Few things are more unappealing than visiting a lovely natural area and finding it marred with toilet paper left by inconsiderate previous visitors.

Sun Protection

Backpackers often interpose a physical barrier between themselves and the sun. They can wear wide-brimmed hats, long-sleeve shirts, and long pants, although the long sleeves and pants will often be too warm. Hikers can also use an umbrella to block the sun, and an opaque ointment such as zinc oxide ointment.

EYEGLASSES CASE?

HEAVY!

LEAVE IT BEHIND!

Sunglasses

with Retaining cord

WRAP it in BANDANNA

WRAP IT IN YOUR HAT!

this is your MULTIUSE CASE!

SUNSCREEN

Between 10:00 A.M. and 4:00 P.M., backpackers should use a broad-spectrum water-resistant sunscreen with a SPF (sun protection factor) of 15 or higher on skin exposed to the sun. Ideally, sunscreen should be applied liberally half an hour before exposure to the sun begins because sunscreen needs to bind to the skin. Even so, sunscreen can still be rubbed off or washed off by water or perspiration, so it should be reapplied every one-and-a-half to two hours. Don't forget your lips! Lip balm with at least SPF 15 will prevent your lips from burning and keep them from chapping at the same time.

SUNGLASSES

Sunglasses should offer 100 percent protection from UVA and UVB rays. Using polarized lenses will eliminate the glare reflected from water and snowfields. "Neutral density gray" lenses can be dark enough to give good solar protection while allowing you to see true colors. If your route includes glacier travel or many snowfields, you'll appreciate having side shields and a nose shield. The side shields dramatically reduce the amount of light reflected from the sides. In addition to offering sun protection, sunglasses can also be used to protect eyes from wind-driven dust and sand. Ultralighters sometimes carry their sunglasses in a soft fleece bag, an extra hiking sock, or some other improvised system. If you have expensive sunglasses, using a sturdy case will give surer protection for very little added weight.

Insect Protection

Backpackers often have to cope with yellow jackets, mosquitoes, biting flies, ticks, fleas, chiggers, and other stinging or biting insects. These bothersome insects can turn a great route or camp into an unpleasant experience. This is especially true for tarp users, who may be kept awake by buzzing, stinging insects at night.

PHYSICAL BARRIERS TO INSECTS

One way to thwart insect pests is to have a physical barrier between you and the insects. The barrier can be clothing, the fabric of a tent, or the mesh of "no-see-um" netting.★ Mosquito netting will keep mosquitoes away from you, but its holes may be large enough to let smaller insect pests through. That's why no-see-um netting was developed. Unfortunately, no-see-um netting has openings so small it can restrict airflow and allow condensation to form on a tent's walls and ceiling. Usually, however, the condensation is preferable to being pestered by insects.

INSECT HEAD NETS

Insect head nets are effective at keeping insects away from the face and head. Head nets are usually worn with a hat underneath to keep the netting from touching the skin. Head nets can even be effective when you're asleep under a tarp at night as long as you are willing to wear a hat while you sleep. If you would rather make a head net than buy one, they can easily be made at home with minimal sewing skills. Be sure to use

wear a hat
with a brim
under a bug head net
when sleeping out
under the stars
This ain't perfect
but it's better'n nuthin'!

★"No-see-um" is one common name for "punkies," or biting midges. These tiny biting flies are so small they can penetrate ordinary mosquito netting.

black or dark netting. White netting can be difficult to see through in bright sunshine. An insect head net can have several secondary uses. In windy conditions it can keep your hat and sunglasses on your head, and if you run out of sunscreen, wearing it will reduce the effect of the sun's burning rays on your face.

PERMETHRIN

Another way to discourage insects is spraying your hiking clothing with Permethrin, a contact insecticide, before your trip. Hang the clothing up outdoors and spray the outer surfaces to moisten them. Pants, shirts, and especially socks should be sprayed. Do not breathe the spray or allow it to contact your skin. Once the Permethrin dries, insects that contact your clothing will leave quickly. Permethrin isn't for use on your skin. For that you'll need insect repellent.

INSECT REPELLENTS

The most commonly used insect repellent that can be applied to skin is DEET. DEET doesn't kill mosquitoes, it confuses them so they a have hard time recognizing you as a target. DEET should not be applied near the eyes or mouth, or over cuts or scrapes. DEET can cause skin rashes in a small percentage of users and it can also damage some plastics and synthetic fabrics. For these reasons, some hikers prefer using volatile plant oils. These oils include citronella oil, rosemary oil, lemongrass oil, peppermint oil, and clove oil. These volatile oils need much more frequent application than DEET (they need to be applied every hour or two), and they are also less effective than DEET.

First-aid Kits
PERSONAL FIRST-AID KIT

Ideally, every hiker should carry a personal first-aid kit to use for their own minor injuries and have training in at least basic first-aid. Carry only first-aid supplies you know how to use. A personal first-aid kit doesn't need to be large or heavy, but it should at least include Band-Aids of different sizes, adhesive or sport tape, several safety pins, personal medications, moleskin, and small scissors. It is much easier to trim and shape moleskin and other first-aid supplies with scissors than with a knife. The scissors on a Swiss Army knife works well enough. The safety pins can turn a long-sleeve shirt or jacket into a sling for an arm. The scissors and safety pins are both useful for other first-aid and non-first-aid purposes as well.

GROUP FIRST-AID KIT

If you are backpacking in a group, it's a good idea to have a group first-aid kit in addition to each person's individual first-aid kit. A group first-aid kit typically contains items that are potentially important, but not important enough to justify being carried by each individual. It can have a larger selection of Band-Aids, some sterile gauze pads, disposable gloves, elastic bandages, triangular bandages, tick tweezers, antibiotic ointment, alcohol swabs, and other supplies.

That may sound like a lot of gear, but it doesn't have to be overly heavy, and can be carried in a fanny pack and rotated to a different group member each time the group stops to rest or eat. When you use something from the kit, keep the empty wrapper with the kit as a reminder to replace it when the trip is over.

Gear Repair Kit

It's helpful and sometimes essential to be able to repair gear that fails in the field. The kit doesn't need to be extensive, expensive, or heavy. A minimal fabric repair kit can consist of just a needle, with dental floss for use as thread. For more sophisticated hand-sewing, a few yards of strong synthetic thread can be wound around a business card and kept in a film canister.

A group gear repair kit can include duct tape, gaffers tape or rip-stop repair tape, cable ties, blanket pins, partial tubes of seam sealer, Shoe-Goo, five-minute epoxy, Silnet for silnylon, and an inflatable-mattress repair kit.

Headlamp

Backpackers need a dependable light to use after dark, and if it can be used hands-free, that's an advantage. For this reason, headlamps are more popular than hand-held flashlights with backpackers.

LED (light-emitting diode) technology has largely replaced incandescent bulbs in headlamps for good reason. LEDs are far more reliable than incandescent bulbs. LEDs also drain less power, allowing batteries to last longer, sometimes over one hundred hours. LEDs can last for thousands of hours.

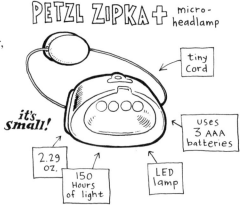

PETZL ZIPKA+ micro-headlamp

it's **Small!**

tiny Cord

uses 3 AAA batteries

2.29 oz.

150 Hours of light

LED lamp

OTHER LED LIGHTS

Tiny LED lights are so light in weight that even ultralighters can carry two of them without feeling over-burdened. If you decide to carry two, you may want to have one white light for observing true colors and a red one to use when you want to preserve your night vision. The red LED light drains even less power from its battery than its counterpart, so it will provide light considerably longer than a white LED.

Whistle

No one expects to become lost or to need to signal others on an outing, but if you do need to signal, a whistle is very effective. A whistle requires less energy than shouting, and its sound carries farther than the human voice. There are "referee" whistles with small round "peas" inside, and there are also "pealess" whistles, which are ear-piercingly shrill even after being dunked in water. Either type is fine for backpacking, although kayakers, canoeists, and others around water will prefer pealess whistles. For others, the main concern is to have a whistle that is loud. In a group, whistles are excellent for signaling a prearranged understanding such as "here's the water hole" or "I found the trail." In an emergency, three blasts on a whistle is a distress signal in the U.S.A., and two blasts is the answer. Nearly everywhere else, six whistle blasts at slow intervals indicate distress, three blasts is the answer, and one or two blasts indicate nonemergency calls.

PART 6

On the Trail

Tips on Sharing Gear

The Lightweighter's Camp

The Quick Start

Tips on Sharing Gear

Sharing "group" items with hiking companions is a great way to lighten individual loads. Sharing the heaviest items is particularly helpful, but any items that can be shared will lighten your load. Good candidates for shared use are the shelter, water filter, stove, camera gear, and guidebooks.

When traveling with your regular sleeping partner, consider sharing a quilt for two, or zip open a single sleeping bag and share it like a quilt. This is efficient, since the two sleepers will keep each other warm. Beware, however, of the dreaded "quilt hog" who leaves you completely uncovered while sleeping soundly, monopolizing the whole quilt.

Serious thought needs to be given to how shared items are distributed between hikers. It does not make sense to have one hiker carry the stove, another carry fuel, and a third carry the pot. If just one of these items is with a hiker who is absent, the other two items are ineffective. It is better to have one person carry the stove, fuel, and pot, and the others contribute by carrying other group gear.

Careful when dividing the group gear

When a shelter is shared, the hikers who are not carrying the shelter should carry a lightweight emergency shelter in case they get separated from the shelter bearer. It can be a poncho, a bivouac sack, a reflective "space blanket," or some other lightweight shelter. This sort of self-sufficiency is also useful when one hiker is injured and can't continue. The main shelter can be used to make the injured hiker and a caregiver comfortable while others go for help using their own individual shelters. It is important that every hiker always be equipped to be able to camp alone safely, in case they become separated from their companions.

The Lightweighter's Camp

Traditional hikers usually use well-established campsites near the trail, and these campsites are often conveniently near a water source. Such sites are relatively large and have been used many times by other campers.

Using an established camp has several disadvantages. It degrades the sense of privacy and solitude for both the camper and passing hikers. Frequently used camps are likely to have at least one established fire ring, and litter will usually be evident. Local animals may associate the area with food scraps left by careless campers.

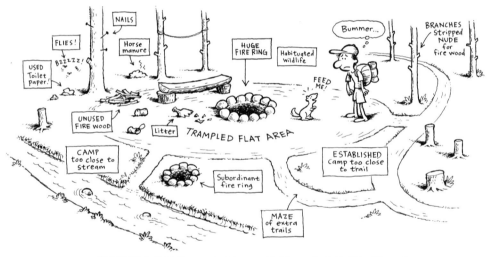

TYPICAL IMPACTED CAMPSITE

Lightweight backpackers usually search for a campsite farther away from the trail than these traditional camps. A hundred yards away from a trail is usually enough to guarantee privacy and seclusion.

Small shelters allow the use of very small campsites. A small wild site well off the beaten path often can be turned into a suitable campsite by moving a downed tree limb or making other minor changes. In such a setting a small shelter in a color that blends with the surroundings may be virtually undetectable.

STEALTH CAMP

This sort of camp was named a "stealth camp" by Ray Jardine.★

A stealth camp will be cleaner and more pristine than an established campsite. Wildlife won't associate this site with easy-to-find food. This is especially true if the camper doesn't cook at the campsite. The hiker's evening meal can be cooked and eaten before a campsite is selected, then the hiker can continue on for an hour or so before establishing camp. This guarantees there won't be cooking smells in camp to lure wildlife to the camp to raid the food supply.

Before leaving the next morning, any changes that were made in the site need to be "undone" to restore the site to its natural condition. This will keep the site from becoming an obvious new campsite.

★Ray Jardine, adventurer and long-distance hiker was one of the first people to recommend running shoes and homemade "sleeping quilts" instead of sleeping bags for long-distance hikers. His book *Beyond Backpacking* details his hiking experiences and philosophy and has been very influential in promoting lightweight backpacking.

The Quick Start

Sometimes it's useful to break camp and start hiking very quickly. Lightweight hikers have the advantage of not having much gear to pack up. The ability to pack up fast is especially useful for leaders who have to deal with all their own camp chores while assisting others.

A quick start requires some planning and preparation even with a small gear kit. To make a quick start, prepare for it the night before. If you have shelter mates, discuss who will be responsible for packing community items, such as the shelter. Everything except the shelter and sleeping system should be packed up before going to sleep. This leaves a minimum of gear to be put away the next morning. With everything ready, all that needs to be done is: Wake up, get up, pack up, and go!

Routines established at home don't have to dictate the patterns followed on the trail. Instead of having breakfast in camp, consider hiking for a while, munching snacks loaded into pockets the night before, and brushing teeth at a midmorning pause.

Hikers who practice the quick start can be hiking just a few minutes after they wake up. By the time others are beginning to peer out of their shelters, the quick starter can be miles ahead, warm from hiking and enjoying a trailside breakfast.

PART 7

Back Home Again

Cleaning and Storing Gear

Cleaning and Storing Gear

When the hike is over, gear should be sorted into three piles: (1) items used daily; (2) items used only once or occasionally; and (3) items that weren't used at all. If the first-aid and gear repair kits are in pile two or three, count your blessings and put them in pile number one. Do the same with the compass, long underwear, warm hat, warm jacket, rain gear, and any other items that are important to safety.

Now, take a good hard look at what is still in piles two and three, and ask, "Is this item really contributing to my comfort and safety?" If it is, put it in pile number one. If it's not, consider not taking it in the future. Do this after every outing and the amount of gear you carry will dwindle to a list that is just right for you.

make sure that down sleeping bags are completely dry after a trip and before storage.

Routine Maintenance

The shelter should be air dried to prevent mildew. The sleeping system needs to be fluffed and hung up to dry. Several days will be needed to completely air dry synthetic insulation. Down may need a week of drying. Some moisture will stay in the insulation after it feels dry to the touch. If you're impatient, put it through a cycle or two of medium heat in a dryer. Then store it uncompressed in a large breathable storage sack.

Water filters need maintenance between outings. Some filter manufacturers recommend pumping a diluted solution of regular household bleach through filters before storage. Check the instructions or contact the manufacturer for maintenance instructions. At the very least, disassemble the filter, rinse it well, and let it air dry.

Water containers should be emptied, washed with mild soap and water, thoroughly rinsed, then stored with their caps off.

Replenish any first-aid supplies that have been used. If you left the empty first-aid wrappers in the first-aid kit, that will remind you of what has been used.

Footgear should be cleaned. Wet footgear needs to dry slowly in a warm, dry place to be in good condition for the next hike. Remove the laces and footbeds. Some hikers sprinkle baking soda inside their boots to help absorb moisture and odors. Crumpled newspaper or shoe trees inside shoes or boots will help them keep their shape as they dry.

Appendix A
Lightweight Hiking Gear List

The most valuable things we take with us into the wilderness are the judgment and knowledge that results from experience and training. No gear list can keep every hiker safe and comfortable under all conditions. The following list includes items that are essential for safe travel at low to moderate elevations from late spring through early fall, in the midlatitudes. It may need to be added to, depending on your particular needs and the expected weather conditions in the area you are visiting.

Think carefully before leaving out items on this list. Unexpected changes in weather and other surprising events are common in any outdoor adventure. A lightweight hiking kit has few redundancies, and little can be spared without incurring unnecessary risk. Inexperienced hikers are often not efficient in their use of gear, and in windy or cool weather some hikers, regardless of experience, simply need more clothing and sleeping insulation than others. Whenever that is the case, those hikers should consider supplementing this list with clothing and equipment they know will work well for them.

GEAR CHECKLIST

This checklist is for a low-elevation late spring, summer, or early fall outing.

Major Items

- ❑ backpack (small, light-weight)
- ❑ shelter (tarp, bivy sack or tent, with stakes)
- ❑ sleeping bag, quilt, or half bag (top loft 1½ to 2 inches)
- ❑ sleeping pad (closed cell, three-quarter length)
- ❑ cooking system (optional): stove, fuel, pot, spoon
- ❑ food with lightweight food bag (twenty-four to thirty-two ounces/day)
- ❑ footgear

Clothing

- ❑ warm hat
- ❑ sun hat
- ❑ shirts
- ❑ torso insulation: two layers (sweater, vest, jacket, parka), ¾-inch total thickness
- ❑ pants
- ❑ leg insulation (synthetic long underwear bottoms)
- ❑ gloves or mittens, over-mitts (optional)
- ❑ socks (at least a pair and a spare)
- ❑ rain gear for torso and head (hooded rain parka or poncho)
- ❑ rain gear for legs (rain pants or rain chaps)

Miscellaneous

- ❑ water containers (four-plus liters recommended capacity)
- ❑ water filter (shared) or chemicals
- ❑ matches and fire starter
- ❑ nylon cord (50 feet)
- ❑ first-aid kit
- ❑ gear repair kit
- ❑ insect repellent
- ❑ head net
- ❑ whistle (loud!)
- ❑ compass
- ❑ map in plastic bag
- ❑ headlamp
- ❑ knife (folding, small)
- ❑ sunglasses and case
- ❑ sunscreen
- ❑ hygiene kit (toothbrush, tooth powder, etc.)

Recommended Reading

Fleming, June. Staying Found: *The Complete Map and Compass Handbook*. Seattle: The Mountaineers, 2001, 158 pages.

Jardine, Ray. *Beyond Backpacking*. La Pine, OR: Adventure Lore Press, 2000, 504 pages.

Meyer, Kathleen. *How to Shit in the Woods*. Berkeley: Ten Speed Press, 1994, 107 pages.

O'Bannon, Allen and Clelland, Mike. *Allen and Mike's Really Cool Backpackin' Book*. Guilford, CT: The Globe Pequot Press, 2001, 162 pages.

Townsend, Chris. *The Backpacker's Handbook*. New York: McGraw-Hill, 1996, 352 pages.

Twight, Mark. *Extreme Alpinism*. Seattle: The Mountaineers, 1999, 240 pages.

Index

first-aid kits
    personal, 80–81, 90
    group, 81
floss, dental, 75
food, 57–69
foot washing, 76–77
footgear, 43–47, 92
    fit, 45–47
flashlight, 81
freeze-dried food, 59, 64
from-the-skin-out weight, 8

G

gear checklist, 94
gear repair kit, 81
gloves, 30

H

half bags, 22
hand washing, 76
hanging food, 68
hard-anodized aluminum
    pots, 64
hats, 27
head nets, 13, 79–80
headlamp, 81–82
hydration systems, 50–56
hygiene kit, 74–75

I

insect protection, 79–80
insulation requirements-sleeping
    system, 20, 21, 22
iodine water treatment, 52–53

J

jacket
    insulated, 28–29
    rain, 39–40

K

knife, 73

L

LED lights, 81–82
leg layers, 29
light-emitting diodes. See LED
    lights
lyophilization, 59

M

map, 74
matches, 72
microfiber towels, 75–76
mittens, 30, 32
mosquito netting, 79
multipurpose items, 3–5

N

no-cook food, 59–60
no-see-um netting, 13, 79
nylon cord, 73

O

odor-barrier bags, 67
oral hygiene, 75
overflow sack, 11
overmitts, 30

P

Pacific Crest Trail food hanging
    method, 68
pack weight, 2–6
pants
    hiking, 29
    rain, 41
parachute cord. See nylon cord
parka, 41

pathogens, 50–54
permethrin, 80
plastic containers for water, 54–56
platypus water bladders, 56
pocket stove. *See* Esbit stove
poles, trekking, 14, 15
ponchos, 3, 37–38
postal scale, 2
pots, 62–64
protozoa, 50–53

Q

quick start, 88
quilts, sleeping, 20–22

R

rain chaps, 38
rain jackets, 39–40
rain parkas, 41
rain pants, 41
rainwear, 33–42
repair kit, 81
running shorts, 29

S

sandals, 44–45
scales, for weighing gear, 2
seam sealer, for silnylon, 12
sediment, 51
sharing gear, 84–85
shelters, 12–17
shirts, 28
silnylon, 12
silt, 51
sleeping bags, 20, 91
sleeping pads, 18–19
sleeping systems, 18–23
soap, biodegradable, 56, 75–76
soccer shorts, 29
socks, 31–32
steam baking, 65–66

storing gear, 90–92
stoves
    alcohol, 61
    compressed-gas, 60
    Esbit, 61–62
    traditional hiker, 60
    Trangia alcohol, 61
    ultralight, 61–62
    white-gas, 60
summit pack, 10
sun hats, 27
sun protection, 78–79
sunglasses, 78–79
sunscreen, 78
synthetic fabrics, 26
synthetic insulation, 21

T

t-shirt, 28
tarps, 12–13
tents, 14–15
titanium pots, 64
toilet paper, 77
toiletries, unscented, 74–75
tooth powder, 75
toothache, 75
toothbrush, 75
toothpaste, 75
topographic map, 74
torso clothing, 28–29, 38–39
trail shoes, 43–47
trekking sandals, 44–45

U

ultralight backpacks, 10–11
ultralight stoves, 61–62
ultraviolet light water treatment,
    53–54
umbrellas, 35–36
United States Geological Survey.
    See map

V

ventilation
    rainwear, 33, 38–40
    tents, 15
vest, insulated, 28–29
viruses, in water, 51

W

water, 50–56
water containers, 54–56
water filters, 51–52

water treatment, 52–54
waterborne pathogens, 50–51
waterproof/breathable rainwear
    fabrics, 34–35
waterproof/nonbreathable rainwear
    fabrics, 35
weighing gear, 2–6
weight, computing, 7–8
whistle, 82
white-gas stoves, 60
wind shirts, 35
wool clothing, 26

Meet the Author

I first met the author at a Grand Tetons hike whose participants included many leaders in the ultralight backpacking "movement." Amid all the guys sporting cutting-edge gear, there was this older guy dressed in simple hiking clothes with a small book bag and a big smile. That guy's name was Don Ladigin.

Don began an active life in the outdoors in 1945 when he first started backpacking as a child with his parents in and around Yosemite Valley. He quickly figured out that carrying a light pack made for an easier hike, and has been refining the technique ever since. As a youngster, Don got used to trip leaders seeing his small pack and grilling him at the trailhead. Did he know the hike ahead would take several days? Was he sure there really was a shelter and a sleeping bag in his tiny pack? Don's answer, invariably, was "yes." In the following decades Don hiked extensively in the United States and internationally. In addition to innumerable private hikes with friends, he served as a leader on many Sierra Club outings and with the Outdoor Pursuits Program at the University of Oregon.

Don Ladigin enjoyed ultralight backpacking before many readers were born. His prowess is evident despite his considerable humility, and his straightforward approach makes for valuable reading.

—Glen "Homemade" Van Peski
Gossamer Gear founder